"A marvelous digest of practical inform.......
ing the imminent death of a family mem.......
follow guide on managing our fears whe.......
than our presence. When words are necessary not only to address difficult decisions
and say goodbyes, but to provide comfort and healing, this exquisite book shows us
that it is possible to find them."

—SANDRA BERTMAN, PH.D., Director, Program of Medical
Humanities, University of Massachusetts Medical School

"This book underscores the fact that saying goodbye is just as much for the living
as for the dying . . . A practical guide to support people so they can engage in some
of life's most difficult conversations. Dr. Wogrin's clear sample scripts provide simple and useful entry points for difficult communications."

—D. RIGNEY CUNNINGHAM, Executive Director,
Hospice & Palliative Care Federation of Massachusetts

"Finding one's way through grief can seem impossible at times. By artfully weav-
ing real stories with practical experience, Carol Wogrin thoughtfully illustrates
how loss and life can coexist."

—SALLY OKUN, Executive Director, Center for Life Care,
Planning & Support

"Full of practical suggestions and clarifying insights. I only wish I could have read
it before my mother died, or sooner in the much longer process of my husband's
struggle with Alzheimer's . . . This is a sorely needed resource for us [Alzheimer's
caregivers], but I value even more the general advice—how to raise the difficult issues, identifying and illuminating our choices, how to make the most of the available opportunities."

—ELISABETH PETERSON, family caregiver

Matters of Life and Death

Matters of Life and Death

FINDING THE WORDS
TO SAY GOODBYE

Carol Wogrin

BROADWAY BOOKS
NEW YORK

Broadway Books titles may be purchased for business or promotional use or for special sales. For information, please write to: Special Markets Department, Random House, Inc., 1540 Broadway, New York, NY 10036.

BROADWAY BOOKS and its logo, a letter B bisected on the diagonal, are trademarks of Broadway Books, a division of Random House, Inc.

Visit our website at www.broadwaybooks.com

Library of Congress Cataloging-in-Publication Data

Wogrin, Carol.
Matters of life and death: finding the words to say goodbye /
Carol Wogrin.—1st ed.
p. cm.
1. Death—Psychological aspects.
2. Interpersonal communication.   I. Title.
BF789.D4 W62 2001
155.9'37—dc21
00-068081

FIRST EDITION

Designed by Jennifer Ann Daddio

ISBN 0-7679-0395-1

1   3   5   7   9   10   8   6   4   2

To Conrad Wogrin,
who taught me to strive
to achieve my goals
and fulfill my dreams

Contents

ACKNOWLEDGMENTS   *xi*

INTRODUCTION   *xiii*

ONE: *Talking with Dying People:*
What Do You Say, What Do You Do?   1

TWO: *Planning Ahead*   31

THREE: *The Dying Process*   57

FOUR: *The "Long Goodbye"*   85

FIVE: *Even Difficult Relationships*
Require Goodbyes   109

SIX: *Helping Children Say Goodbye*   134

SEVEN: *Lessons from the Dying*   169

RESOURCES   183

Acknowledgments

First and foremost, I want to thank Pat Boland for her involvement and enthusiasm every step of the way. Without her, this book would have never been written. She played many roles, from coming up with the initial idea for the book, working as my agent, and providing careful editing and thoughtful feedback throughout each chapter. Her constant question of "When do you think you'll have it done?" kept me writing at times when I would have been more inclined to put the whole project away. She is an integral part of this book.

I want to thank my editors at Broadway, initially Tracy Behar and Angela Casey, then later, Trish Medved. Each gave her careful attention and valuable feedback. This book is much better for all of their work.

My sister, Nancy Confrey, my sister-in-law, Beth Kiendl, and my friend Devorah Steinberg each read various chapters and gave feedback that molded the book. Their suggestions were extremely helpful, and their encouragement kept me writing. I also want to thank my friend Ken Wasiniak for coming up with the title for this book.

My husband, Morey Goodman, and children, Dan, Jeff, Andy, and Dylan, shared their excitement over the idea of me writing a book, showed their tolerance as I struggled my way through it, and, in general, have kept my life from ever being dull. And also, a special thank-you to my close friend Stephanie Danforth, who helps sustain me and who, even when things seem dark, keeps me laughing.

Finally, I want to thank all of the people I've worked with over the years, who have let me into their lives, taught me about life, death, and the strength of the human spirit in the face of unbelievable adversity. They have given me far more than they probably know. Thank you.

Introduction

I began working with children with cancer, renal failure, and other life-threatening illnesses as a nurse in the mid 1970s. As a new nursing graduate, the high-tech unit of cancer care and seriously ill children seemed exciting and challenging. As it turned out, it wasn't the critical care, medical technology, or cutting edge treatment that drew me deeper into the work. It was the children and their families. Early on in my career, I learned about the privilege of being allowed to share in some of the most meaningful experiences in people's lives.

I also learned how frightening it can feel to talk about death when it appears to be a reality, and how rewarding it is for people who meet that challenge, and respond in ways *other* than pulling away.

After a decade of working as a nurse, I went on for training as a psychologist. Over the years, I have had the opportunity to work in many different settings, and with people of all ages, as they face the end of their lives, and the end of the lives of those they love. I have interacted with them as they felt the grief that follows a loss, and the losses that accompany serious illness, including the ultimate loss of a person to death.

It is the individuals and the families who have let me into their lives that have been my finest teachers. Teachers not only about death, but more important, teachers about what is important in life. This book is primarily about the lessons I have learned from many different people who have had to struggle with this all important feature of life that we too often avoid: Life is impermanent, fragile, and very precious.

Coming up against our own fears and vulnerabilities is never an easy task. Death is not an easy topic for many to address because we don't like the fact that it exists—for us or for the people we love. Who doesn't know the experience of wanting to pull away from others when we feel helpless, or don't know what to say in the face of something unwanted that we can't change?

We all need to learn the importance of creating, and using the opportunities we have while we still have them. Today may be all we have—either for ourselves or with someone we love. But our relationships and experiences are complex, and there is no single or right way to incorporate a discussion of illness and death into our lives.

How do you talk about death, and join with those you love in making end-of-life decisions, when you are addressing these strong feelings in real relationships, not just as abstract concepts? This book will walk you through the process of making choices about your words, and your actions, when someone you love is dying.

There is no prescription for what to do and say, and no one right way to go about caring for, and comforting, a dying person. This book offers suggestions about words and phrases you might want to use or modify in order to start difficult or uncomfortable conversations. The book addresses relationships that have always been close, as well as those that have been marked by poor communication from the beginning. Use the book as a guide that can help you manage your fears—the fear of saying the wrong thing, of upsetting others, of facing overwhelming feelings—at a time when you have your last chances to say what you want, to those you love.

In this book you will read the stories of many people caring for someone they love as they near death. Some of the stories are compilations of common experiences we all share as we near death, but most of the stories are from people I have known, though I have changed the names and identifying details for the purpose of maintaining anonymity. Occasionally, at the request of the person who shared their experience, I have used real names.

Since the experiences that surround death apply to men and women equally, I have alternated between the use of "he" and "she." The choice of "he" or "she" at different times is not ever meant to assign the issue being discussed to that gender.

There are many good books available that describe the emotional, psychological, and medical aspects of dying, death, and grief. The focus of this book is finding the words to address these experiences as they arise, and making important, end-of-life choices consciously.

We need to develop the skill of communicating with the dying—through talking and nonverbal expression—in order to offer comfort, both emotional and physical. It is time we begin talking about death, so the end of life is as rich and fulfilling as the rest, and so we can be there for those we love, when they need us the most.

ONE

Talking with Dying People: What Do You Say, What Do You Do?

The most essential thing in life is to develop an
unafraid, heartfelt communication with others, and it is
never more important than with a dying person.
—SOGYAL RINPOCHE

Death is a guaranteed part of all our lives—the deaths of people we love, as well as our own death. The question is not *whether* we face death or not, but rather, *how* we face it. Despite the fact that death is an inevitable experience for everyone, many of us still, when confronted with an impending death, unconsciously react with avoidance to our strong feelings of fear and sadness. Few of us have learned to develop a facility for talking about death, or talking with dying people.

The Value of Saying Goodbye

Grieving begins as soon as you get the news about a serious illness or the impending death of someone you love, and continues long after their death. The art of saying goodbye really begins at this time of first knowing the person you love will be leaving your world.

Our relationships with people who are dying *are* different, and do have a special poignancy that others don't. You may have only a week to say goodbye, or you may have years, but it is your acute awareness that their life is now time-limited, and your relationship with them also time-limited, that gives you both the opportunity to interact differently.

One of the most important tasks in moving through the grief process is shifting from interacting with the dying person in your *external* world, to holding them entirely in your *internal* world—in your thoughts, memories, and feelings, and in your very identity. Saying goodbye, in words and actions, helps clarify your feelings about what a particular relationship has meant to you, and lays the groundwork for the process of making this shift. When you take the time, and make the effort to say a conscious goodbye, you will know the person you love better, and you will know yourself better.

Why Is It Important to Say Goodbye, in Words or Actions?

When hit with a loss as large as a death, you inevitably are left with many difficult feelings—sadness, anger, regret, sometimes depression. The grief process, which involves making sense of these feelings, coping with them, and reworking them, always takes a lot of time. The specific feelings you have, and the intensity of the different feelings, will be partially determined by the way you use the time you have when the person you care about is dying. Saying goodbye, in words or in actions, can give you the opportunity to share your love for another clearly and deliberately.

Generally, when you are careful and conscious in what you say and do in the final years, months, and days of a person's life, you will have fewer regrets after they die; you won't be agonizing over what you should or could have said in the past. A thoughtful goodbye can also give you the opportunity to resolve old conflicts that have long gone unaddressed, and leave the relationship feeling more complete.

Relationships are built on experiences shared *between* two people. It is only logical that you need an ending to a relationship that takes place between yourself and another person. When you don't take the opportunity to say goodbye, you will likely be left with the challenge of working through a relational process entirely on your own. This is a much more difficult task.

Being able to join and support a person in their final phase of life, and talk with them about what their life has been, who they have been to you, and how they will remain with you is of vital importance in working through this process. This joining and sharing will take different forms in different relationships, depending on the personalities involved.

Many of your thoughts and feelings after a death—whether or not you feel regret at things left unsaid or unexpressed—

have to do with aspects of your own behavior that involved a choice for you. Usually, after someone close to you dies, you think about who you were in the relationship, what you did or didn't do, say, give, or what you did and didn't share while you had the chance.

You may be so used to avoiding awkward or highly charged emotional situations that you find yourself completely overwhelmed by strong feelings when you learn someone you love is going to die. This is normal. But if you respond to those feelings by withdrawing or freezing up emotionally, you will not be able to talk to the dying person. You may miss the last opportunity of a lifetime.

The Power of Secrets

Honesty is an important aspect of relationships, and certainly necessary if we want to be close to someone. This is especially true when we are dealing with times as significant as the impending end of someone's life—the final opportunity to be close to him. However, all too often during this emotionally difficult time, the importance of honesty seems to be forgotten, and people act instead on their desire to "protect" loved ones from emotional pain. Rarely does this approach actually help the person. Usually, they are left more isolated and alone.

MR. JOHNSON

Years ago, I had an experience that impressed upon me the extent to which well-intended secrets can cause pain at the end of life. During college, I worked the night shift in a community hospital as a nurse's aide. In this role I was usually assigned to the jobs that the unit nurses least wanted to do.

On this particular night, Mr. Johnson was dying. Mr. Johnson had, reportedly, always been a very proud and private man. He was quite elderly, was bleeding from his intestines, and due to complex medical problems, little could be done to stop it. The previous afternoon, his daughters, with the encouragement of his doctor, had made the decision to withhold this information from him. They believed they could shield him from unnecessary distress by withholding the information that he was dying. The doctor said his death would be fairly rapid, so it seemed kind to spare him this devastating news.

His daughters left at the end of visiting hours, as they were required to do in those days. With "cheerful" assurances, they told him they would see him tomorrow. When I came on duty near midnight, I was apprised of the situation and assigned to spend the night at his bedside. I was given very specific instructions on what not to say. He was not to be told that he was dying. Worse still, he was not told that he was bleeding, since he was, of course, bright enough to understand the consequence of uncontrolled bleeding.

All night long, Mr. Johnson was on and off the bedpan, thinking his bowels were very loose. During the first half of the night, he got increasingly angry at the fact that no one would give him anything to treat his condition. I stood mute as he yelled at me. The nurses, who were all uncomfortable with the situation, avoided the room like the plague. As the night progressed and he got weaker, he could not always make it to the bedpan. His anger turned to shame. Had he known he was bleeding, the situation would have been much more tolerable. Adults don't feel shame when they can't control bleeding. They do feel ashamed when they can't control their bowels. He became quieter, more apologetic, and more withdrawn each time I cleaned him up. I could offer no true support, because I was little other than a witness to his loss of control. At eight o'clock in the morning, after an active and productive life, Mr. Johnson died, ashamed and alone.

Even at the time, I understood what a tragedy this was. Mr. Johnson was a competent man. He had led a life with much to be proud of. He had daughters who loved and respected him. Out of love, their own fears of death, and feelings of helplessness, they followed advice that they believed would make his final hours easier. The result was cruelly opposite. This independent man was stripped of all choice about how he would say goodbye. His distorted view of the situation caused him to spend his final hours feeling badly about himself. His daughters, also, had no opportunity to say goodbye to their father. The last interactions his daughters were able to have with him were those of pretense.

Secrets are very meaningful. They influence how close, or not close, you feel. They determine who's in and who's out. Think of the effect secrets have, even when they are in the service of something good or fun. When planning for a surprise party, for example, there is a time when those doing the planning exclude the person who the party is for. The person the party is for may have a sense something is going on, but doesn't know what. This is all fine, of course, because it is minor, done with good intent, and with an end point to the exclusion. When the party happens, the recipient will, hopefully, enjoy the result.

But, as in Mr. Johnson's case, when you keep secrets about an illness, they have many of the same consequences, only without the happy ending. The person who is excluded probably has a sense that something is going on, but doesn't know what. Or he may have a good idea of what is going on and get the message that no one is willing to talk with him about it.

People may decide to keep information about a very poor prognosis from an ill parent or spouse, believing that they are being kind by sparing them the pain of knowing. Unfortunately, though, that person is now excluded. The people who know will be putting their energy into pretending. Their actions and emotions will be different than what they are saying. While they try to pretend that things are fine, their emotions will show in some way, whether it's through tension, sadness, a false cheerfulness, or avoidance.

Usually, the dying person knows they are dying, even when not told, and they get the message loud and clear that it is not to be spoken about. As a result, a wall is created between people at the very time that closeness is most needed.

What Is a "Good Death"?

Not all people need the same thing or achieve their needs in the same way. Some people like to talk about everything in great detail. The more they share verbally, the closer the bond. Discussions about events, impressions, thoughts, and feelings are central to interactions. For others, talking about feelings and intimate details of life feels very uncomfortable or unnecessary, and it is the sharing of experiences, pursuing common goals, or participating in events together that is the foundation for caring relationships. Still others define their relationships by the degree that they know that someone will be there in times of need—the person who knows you well enough to anticipate what you need and provide it when necessary.

This range of personality styles is equally seen in the ways that people approach death. From the popular writings of Elisabeth Kübler-Ross in the 1970s the idea of a "good death" emerged. Unfortunately, in our desire to figure out a "right" way of dealing with death, we ended up defining the idea of a "good death" very narrowly. The "good death" is often thought to be one in which family members gather together and talk about the impending death—fears, feelings, and plans. Family members talk about things that have gone unsaid for many years; everyone's feelings are understood; and long-standing conflicts are resolved. All who are closely involved have worked through their feelings of anticipatory grief to the point of peaceful acceptance.

This scenario of openness about the death, and about all the complicated feelings that go along with it does happen sometimes, though in my experience, not very often. It certainly is a "good death." However, it is not the only type of death that is "good." There are many ways to come together in final days, to support the person who is dying, to reflect on his or her life and the relationship, and to share what needs to be shared. You can accomplish your goal of being supportive and saying your goodbyes in many different ways—probably as many different ways as there are relationships.

People die the way they live. We do not usually change drastically when we are facing a crisis or major life event. If someone is demanding, bossy, or cranky throughout their life, they are probably going to die demanding, bossy, and cranky. There is the occasional dying person who opens up in a way they never have, and, in a dramatic way, is able to patch up problematic relationships or build relationships where there was previously little emotional connection. This, however, is rare. For most people, the growth that takes place in the final stage of life is simply the next step in their lives, and not a giant leap to becoming someone very different than they were.

Likewise, we should not expect ourselves to change drastically to meet some preconceived idea of the way we "should be" when a friend or family member is dying. If you have always been very private about your emotions, you are probably not going to pour out your innermost feelings because of an impending death. If you have always been very expressive and emotive, you are, most likely, not going to suddenly become very quiet, calm, or stoic in the final time you have to share with someone. If a family's way of engaging with each other has been through arguing and struggling, this is probably the style that will continue.

You are who you are. Part of who we all are, however, is someone who can grow. You can stop and look at the ways you hold yourself back, and find new ways of communicating, either in words or in actions.

To say goodbye find ways to negotiate not only your own feelings, but also the different personality styles in your relationships. It is often easier to accomplish this task among your close friends, who tend to be like you in many ways—either in personality or values. They are people with whom you have *chosen* to be connected.

Negotiating the task with people from the family you grew up in—parents, siblings, close grandparents, aunts, or uncles, however, may be much more difficult. You don't choose your family members and you may be very different from them in personality, values, and life view. Everyone in a family has their role, based on position in the family and individual personality. Commonly, different people in the family carry out different aspects of the family system, with different people being more or less emotional, logical, responsible, fun-loving, impulsive, conservative. Siblings in a family may run the gamut from the "successful one" to the "black sheep."

Figuring out how to bridge the gap between someone who is very emotionally oriented and someone who is very cognitively oriented can be challenging at best, but you will be ahead if you can at least recognize your own preferred style of interaction, and that of the dying person. Accept and work with each other as you are, and find the possibilities inherent in that combination.

PREPARING TO SAY GOODBYE—BETSY

When Betsy's mother called in early January to tell her that her father had cancer, she almost couldn't believe it. She hadn't seen her father in nearly a year, since she and her family were back East for vacation the spring before. He had been so healthy and active then, spending most of every day at the beach with her kids.

At the time of the phone call her parents sounded optimistic. The cancer was caught early and it hadn't spread, or so they thought. Betsy called regularly, but her parents didn't tell her much. They usually just said that he was doing fine. At times she suspected they were downplaying the problems.

Looking back, Betsy thought she had gone along with it because she didn't want her father to be sick, and she didn't want to deal with the disruption his illness would cause in her life. Sometimes her father hadn't sounded good or her mother sounded worried, but Betsy didn't push it when they said the problems were minor. She had offered to fly home to help out several times, but had always been relieved when her mother declined—it would be so much easier to visit in the summer when her children were out of school. Also, she had already arranged for several weeks off from work in July.

Then her mother called in March to say she should come home quickly. The cancer had spread and her father was going downhill fast. They were stopping all treatments other than pain medication. Betsy knew her parents well enough to know they would never request this unless he was doing very poorly.

Her mother met her at the airport. She looked exhausted and older than Betsy remembered. After initial greetings, they said little on the trip back to the house. Seeing how worn-down her mother looked, Betsy felt guilty that she hadn't been back before this.

"I want you to be prepared, Betsy," her mother told her. "Your father looks very different than he did when you last saw him. He's lost a lot of weight." Betsy asked her mother why she didn't tell her sooner that things were going so badly. Her mother said they didn't want to worry Betsy. "You're so busy with your family and your job. And there's not much you could have done from so far away."

Betsy was nervous when they arrived at the house. She walked in behind her mother, determined to appear composed. The first thing she saw was her father lying on the living room couch. She wasn't sure if her gasp had been audible. The reality of his dying hit her. He was so thin! There was almost no resemblance to the burly man she had always known. His skin was drawn over his face, and he had an oxygen tube running into his nose. His skinny arm trembled slightly as he reached out for her. He had lost all of his hair from the chemotherapy treatments. Somehow her legs supported her as she walked across the room to greet him. She hugged him, but didn't know what to say—he looked so fragile!

"Hi, Dad. How are you feeling?"

"Okay," he said, "I've had a pretty good day today."

"Let me go put my suitcase in the bedroom," she said, wanting to get out of the room quickly. As she sat in the bedroom, Betsy realized she felt more like a ten-year-old than a competent woman of almost forty. She felt shocked, helpless, and guilty—why hadn't she come sooner? She told me that, even though she had never been particularly religious, she asked God: "Help me get through this." She struggled to compose her thoughts. She and her father, although close in a certain way, were never very open with each other about very personal or emotional issues. All she could really think was "What on earth am I going to say to him when I walk back into that room?"

WE HAVE VERY FEW ROLE MODELS
FOR DEALING WITH DEATH

Betsy, like most of us, had few role models for dealing with death. We learn through all kinds of blatant and subtle messages that the subject of death is taboo, and to be avoided. If that is all we learn, we are likely to react with avoidance. This was the situation with Betsy. She responded with relief to her mother's assertions that everything was fine—even though she suspected it wasn't—and when she did finally see her parents as her father neared his death, she had to grapple with feelings of guilt over having chosen avoidance.

By keeping death a forbidden subject, you lose your ability to share yourself with people you love when they are dying. Like Betsy, you can be left not knowing what to say or what to do. Then, in response to your own discomfort, you will likely pull away from the dying and from those who are grieving. You avoid them if possible—crossing the street before coming face-to-face, or coming up with endless reasons why today isn't a good day to call. When you can't avoid contact, you may avoid the topic, filling the air with meaningless chatter, acutely aware of what isn't being said.

You may tell yourselves you are being considerate—by not "reminding" the person of their painful experience, not broaching a topic that the person may not want to talk about, not intruding on their privacy. Or you may be brave enough to ask, "How are you?" but because the person can sense your discomfort, they will not be honest, both to spare your intense feelings, and theirs. "Fine," they will respond. You breathe a sigh of relief and change the subject to other trivial and less threatening things.

ACCOMMODATE TO DIFFERENT WISHES, TIMING, AND VIEWPOINTS

A goodbye, like all other aspects of relationships, means that you may need to let go of your expectations of what you would like to see happen, and respect the messages you are getting from the dying person. Today's elderly parents are likely to have very different ideas about the expression of feelings, and be more reticent to talk about death than their adult children are. They grew up in a different time and, in ways, live in a different world. Throughout this book, you will read stories of people who have learned to accommodate different approaches to death.

A dying person might do their best to avoid all direct discussion of death, while their adult children can think of little else, and would love to be able to talk about it openly. Or a seriously ill person might wish very much to be able to talk about their fears and feelings, but those around are determined to talk only about getting better. There is no single way to handle these differences.

MAKE CONSCIOUS CHOICES

Learn to negotiate the differences and make conscious choices about what you express and how you express your thoughts and feelings, instead of avoiding the words or actions entirely because you are afraid and uncomfortable.

Generally, we all like to have rules or clear guidelines about what is right and wrong—they make things much easier and less anxiety-provoking. We want to know the "right thing" to do or say when someone we love is dying. When it comes down to it, only you can answer the question of what you should say—and you will answer this question differently in different situations and relationships. The following are some ideas and guidelines that can help you answer the question when it arises.

Talk About Death

Talking about your feelings makes them much clearer. Feelings and thoughts are very fluid, and we don't necessarily stop and really pay attention to them. When you put them into words, you force yourself to pin them down, and focus on them. The result is twofold. First of all, when you state or write out your feelings, you are putting them into a form that you can listen to or read, which may help to clarify them.

As a psychologist, I often hear people say, as they describe various experiences they are struggling with, "I never realized this before, but . . ." By putting feelings into words, you are able to reflect on them and develop new understandings. This is a primary reason that journal writing is so helpful for so many people.

Second, when you put thoughts and feelings into words, you are usually expressing them to someone else. As long as thoughts remain privately in your own head, you are only able to see them from your own perspective. By talking them through with another person, you can develop a dialogue that will often open you up to new perspectives and new understandings. Sometimes you learn that feelings you have judged as abnormal or shameful are shared by others and are not abnormal at all. By opening yourself, you have the opportunity to learn that feelings you expected to be overwhelming may be far more manageable than you previously thought.

Contrary to popular opinion, thinking and talking about death is not morbid or depressing. Quite the opposite. In order to fully engage in life, you have to engage with one of life's defining characteristics—that it *is* time-limited. Raising your awareness of the reality of life's fragile and transient nature is a major step toward a more conscious valuing of life and life's choices.

It is *always* difficult to be comfortable with that which is unfamiliar. In addition to being largely unexplored in our Western culture, loss and death have very strong feelings attached to them. It is painful to lose someone you love. No matter what your religious or spiritual beliefs, you miss them when they are no longer in your daily life, and it hurts to look toward the future and know they won't be present to share it with you. The combination of very strong, painful feelings, and the common discomfort with the unknown, can be *very* difficult to manage.

Also, the idea of death taps into very deep feelings of vulnerability and helplessness. The reality of our human existence is that we are vulnerable all of the time. Not one of us truly knows if we will be alive tomorrow. But in ways that are very healthy and helpful, we don't walk around constantly experiencing this fact. It would be immobilizing if we did. When someone we know is dying or has died, however, we will be confronted with the tenuousness of life, and will feel intense feelings of vulnerability and helplessness.

Supporting someone as they die, and saying a fulfilling goodbye, is not based on your ability to *overcome* your feelings of vulnerability and lack of control. This isn't very likely. What is both possible and very important, however, is learning to *tolerate* these feelings. This shift in focus can be very empowering. Now you can deal with your feelings, rather than focusing your energy on trying to control whether or not you have uncomfortable feelings.

Ask Yourself: How Do People Who Are Terminally Ill Feel?

Start by trying to imagine yourself in the dying person's position. Think about what it might be like to know that your life is probably ending very soon. Think about leaving behind your partner, children, parents, and friends. How does it feel to face physical deterioration, possible loss of control over your bodily functions, loss of independence, and, possibly, pain? These thoughts are the same for the person you love; regardless of how they are acting, you can be sure that there is much pressing on their minds.

Each person faces their death in their own way. There are, however, some aspects of the dying experience that are common to many, and helpful to understand, in order to support the people you love as they face their deaths. A little knowledge can be helpful to hang on to and use to bind your own anxiety as you struggle with the helplessness you feel in the face of death.

There are plenty of people who have little fear of death itself, but most people have fears about the dying process. Part of what people fear in dying is being alone. You have probably had the experience of having others pull away when you are having a difficult time. Some people avoid you. Others try to "fix" things for you, often by offering platitudes that minimize the importance of what you are trying to cope with. Either way, the result is the same. You are left alone to cope with whatever it is that you are facing.

People expect others to withdraw when they are trying to cope with death. They will often try to shield those around them from their pain, fearing that expressing their sadness, vulnerability, and helplessness will drive others away. Silence from other people will reinforce these beliefs, confirming for them that no one wants to hear about their struggles.

When someone is terminally ill, they are facing a tremendous amount of loss. They know their time with people they love is coming to an end. They are losing everything they hoped their future would hold. Hopes and dreams that aren't yet achieved are coming to a close. They will also be reflecting on what their life has been. And they will worry about the people they are leaving behind, knowing that their loved ones will be in much pain as they grieve.

We spend our lives becoming independent and increasing our skill at taking care of ourselves. Terminal illness threatens to reverse this gained independence. When people are living with serious illness, they are generally facing physical debilitation. They may lose the ability to take care of their physical needs, becoming dependent on others for aspects of daily life they have managed on their own since childhood. They often fear that as the illness progresses, they will be in physical pain. Depending on the disease, people might be facing the loss of their mental competence. In a society that values control as much as ours does, it's not hard to imagine just how frightening potential loss of physical or mental control might be.

More than anything else, people who are terminally ill need to know that those around them, particularly the people they love, will be there with them. They need the people who love them to respond to their physical and emotional needs. They need family and friends to sit with them, to listen to the stories of their past, and their sadness about losing their future. They need people to hear fears and feelings without trying to "fix" things that don't have a remedy. In short, they need the people they love to help carry the emotional load, to assure them their life has had meaning, and that this meaning will continue on after their death. They also need to know that, although the people they love will be grief-stricken, they will, in the long run, be all right.

Remember that actions speak louder than (or at least as loudly as) words. If you try to pretend you feel differently than you do, others will know you are pretending. If you try to

seem cheerful or optimistic when you're not, or try to minimize their fears or concerns with the intention of taking away
their worries, all you will accomplish is building a wall between the other person and yourself. You can't support someone from the other side of a wall.

There are a number of excellent books devoted to describing the needs and experiences of people who are dying.
Several that I particularly recommend are listed in the
Resources section at the end of this book. Getting more familiar with the experiences of people as they die can allay some
of your fears of helplessness as you stand by their sides.

There Is Tremendous Value in Talking About Your Feelings

When you censor your feelings and avoid talking, or even
thinking about them, they, of course, *do* feel unmanageable.
When you can't sort out your feelings and fears, they can be
very confusing and frightening. You'll likely be left only with
this vague sense of dread, which can make you even more intent on avoiding the whole experience.

Don't expect that you will feel completely comfortable in
dealing with or talking about death—you probably won't
achieve this. It's okay to be uncomfortable. Death stirs up
many intense and difficult feelings—on some level, we all
know the people we love will die and we will die ourselves.
That's not an easy thought. However, you *will* be able to tolerate the intense feelings that come up. Learn to be patient with
yourself and to trust your ability. Write in a journal, talk to a
trusted friend, talk to a professional. Use your supports to do

this. Remember, you will not be able to offer support to someone else if you don't understand how to use support yourself, and you will not be able to tolerate difficult feelings in other people if you can't tolerate your own.

Putting your fears into words diminishes their power to some degree. Talking about your fears takes them out of the realm of the unknown and the unmanageable. Once you can speak about your fears and feelings, you have taken the first step in figuring out how to manage them or give them the necessary outlets.

Saying goodbye is as much about life as it is about death. One reason death is so difficult is that it means losing a life that has been important. What has this person's life been, and specifically, who have they been to you? How have they touched your life and what is the legacy they leave with you— how will they live on in you and others? Answering these questions and sharing these answers is the crux of the work to be done.

Finally, take the time to ask yourself, "Have I said what I wanted to say?" Of course, you can never predict how any interaction will progress, and that is the magic of human relationships. But if you do take the time to pay attention to your feelings, sort them out, and review them, you will be better able to plan a path toward action, and say what you would like to say.

No One Has Ever Died from Crying

People are not harmed by normal grief or anger that has appropriate outlets. Grief that is expressed hurts, but does not harm you. It is the grief and intense emotion that has no direct outlet that can cause much harm—affecting everything, including your physical health, your relationships, your ability to tolerate emotions, and your belief in yourself. The idea that you have control over whether you *feel* certain emotions or not, such as anger, sadness, or guilt, is an absolute myth! These feelings are, quite simply, part of the human condition.

What you do have some control over is whether or not you pay attention to your feelings and how you act on them. When you push feelings away, consciously or unconsciously, they wait, unchanged. You use energy keeping them at bay. At some point, these feelings are likely to be tapped by another loss or some other emotionally demanding experience. When this happens, you will usually be flooded by your feelings, which will seem overwhelming, confusing, and "out of line" with what you are currently dealing with.

MELANIE

Thirty-two-year-old Melanie was soft-spoken, and shared little during the first few caregiver support group meetings. She sat with her arms folded tightly across her chest, her legs crossed, and her foot jiggling rapidly. Her face was drawn and she looked exhausted. Most of her discussions with others were about day-to-day caregiver issues, and managing the many demands placed on her as she tried to care for her ill father while still meeting her professional responsibilities. In response to the tears of others, she talked about the fact that she never cried. "I don't know why," she said. "I love my father, and can't even bear to think of him not getting better, but it's like the feelings just aren't there."

During the fourth session, one of the women in the group was talking about the worsening condition of her spouse. Melanie burst into tears. The group was silent for a few minutes, not knowing quite how to react to this change in her behavior.

"I'm okay," she said after a bit. "I've been crying on and off for the past few days. My father has been getting sicker, and I don't think he has much time left. It's actually been a relief in ways . . . crying, I mean. I don't know why I didn't before this." She thought for a minute. "I think I was afraid that if I started I'd never be able to stop."

Saying Goodbye

It is important that you take the time for reflection on what this person has meant to you, and how you would like to offer, and participate in, a final goodbye. Saying goodbye often includes reviewing the past, expressing feelings, and talking about the future. There are several approaches that can be helpful in saying goodbye. Try them out, modify or combine them to fit the needs of the person you love and yourself. What isn't helpful at one time may be just what is needed at another. If your efforts are driven by love, concern, and honest effort, you can't go too far wrong. It is when you are responding primarily to fears about your own painful feelings that you are more likely to get into trouble.

EXTEND THE INVITATION

Start by inviting the person you love to talk about their experience—how they feel physically and emotionally. What is most important for the dying person to express, or do at this point in their lives? Ask yourself if there is some way you can help them with this, and keep in mind that the dying person is probably overwhelmed with feelings of how to leave this world—emotionally and physically.

You may be able to help them with this task, simply by offering. "Is there anything you would like me to do for you after you are gone?" "Is there anything you would like to tell me that you haven't already?" You may be able to be more specific because of what you've noticed: "I noticed that you seemed really sad yesterday when the kids were visiting," or what you know: "I remember that before Dad died, you both said you wanted _____ at your service. Do you still want that?"

You can ask general questions or make comments in gentle ways that encourage discussion about the subject of death.

- "Dad, you seemed a little sad this morning. How are you feeling about being so sick?"
- "I know this must be hard for you. Do you want to talk about it?"
- "Grandma, I love you. Is there anything you want to talk about?"
- "You've gotten so sick this last month, and it makes me sad to see you suffering. How are you managing this?"

Let it be known that you want to talk about it if they are able. If you ask, "How are you?" sit down and wait for an answer. If you get the perfunctory "Fine," ask for a little more. If the person truly doesn't want to say any more, they will make that clear. Often, they are going on the assumption that no one really wants to hear more, and will welcome the sincere indication that you do.

Sharing honest observations you have, such as "You seem quiet today," or "It seems like there's a lot on your mind today," makes it clear that you are interested and willing to listen, without pushing the person to talk about things they don't want to. Statements like "It seems like fighting this illness is wearing you down," leave the door open to talk about many things if they want to. They can talk about how they feel at the moment—either physically or emotionally. They can talk about the bigger picture and how they want you to support them in it. Or they may want to talk only about determination and hope, at which point you can share any honest feelings you have about hopes or fears for the future.

If the answer you get is that she doesn't feel good, whether physically or emotionally, don't immediately try to fix things. Give them time to tell you what they mean. Think about what they are saying. Is the problem one that has a quick solution, or is it one that needs to be voiced so that they are not alone in their experience? If it is a problem with a quick solution, such as the need for a change in pain medication or a back rub to relieve muscle aches, fine, fix it. But if it is a larger problem, sit tight. Let them know that you hear what they are saying. When you can stay with your feelings of helplessness, you are no longer helpless. You are at a point where you can help them be less alone with their feelings. Sharing the load is the greatest gift you can give to someone carrying a heavy burden.

If an invitation to talk is accepted, you also have an opportunity to offer your own feelings. It's fine to let them know that you, too, have fears, intense feelings, or often feel helpless. It is also important to let them know that you can manage these feelings and will find and utilize the supports that you need over time. Remember, your reassurances will only mean something if they are honest. You owe it to yourself and your loved one to take care of yourself.

More than anything else, your ability and willingness to listen is paramount to the quality of the final time you spend with the person you love. Sitting quietly with a dying person—which also means sitting quietly with yourself—is a tremendous service. By being present, quiet, and still, you make room for the person you love to express themselves in whatever way they want or need to. It is probably the clearest way to give the message that you can tolerate and even welcome the feelings that the impending death is stirring up for both of you, and that you are there for them.

EXTEND THE INVITATION IN DIFFICULT RELATIONSHIPS

Sometimes part of what makes sitting with someone difficult, is conflicted feelings in the relationship. This is often the case in relationships with parents. We love them because they are our parents and the attachment is very deep. However, our personalities may be very different, or they may have had problems of their own that got in the way of the warm, supportive relationship we so longed for. There may be a long history of misunderstandings.

When you have strong feelings of ambivalence in a relationship, saying goodbye is particularly hard. If an important relationship is tense, and you do want to say goodbye, but are having a tough time sorting out your feelings, find someone, often a professional therapist, with whom you can talk through your many feelings and get help making choices. You may need to make choices about which feelings or aspects of the relationship you're going to attend to now, and which you are going to put off until later.

Think these decisions through carefully. Use your supports in doing so, either friends, other close family members, or a therapist. Chapter Five of this book addresses, in greater detail, saying goodbye when relationships are very difficult.

DIRECT DISCUSSION

You may suspect that the dying person is not getting what she needs in terms of support, or comfort, but not know what your role should be, or how to approach this in discussion. You can be direct with her and simply ask, "Is there anything you would like to talk about?" "I know this must be a really scary and difficult time, do you feel like you are getting the support you need?" In this way, you can open the door for her to ask for more help to relieve any physical pain, or emotional pain. For example, she may want to talk with a priest, or rabbi, or other spiritual adviser.

When you clearly extend invitations, you will have a good sense of whether she wants to talk about her impending death. Being able to talk directly with her about all that is going on gives you the best opportunity for clear understanding.

If you are able to talk openly, you will likely, over time, address many topics and a range of emotions. What you focus on at any given moment will vary tremendously. We all have normal, intense feelings about death. Allow yourself to express the varied feelings you have—sadness, anger, guilt, helplessness. Sometimes you or the dying person will need to talk about death, the beliefs, and fears you or they have about dying. It is helpful to make plans for after the death—wakes, funerals, burials, cremations. Knowing someone's wishes for the rituals surrounding their death will make decisions that come later easier. And if she is able to state her wishes for what she would like after she dies, these rituals will feel like they include and more fully honor her life.

Other times the focus will be the opposite. The lighter side of life will enter some days, and you might talk about hopes and plans for a more extended future. Ideally, make a lot of room to talk about what has been important in her life, to both you and her. Ask if she would like to document aspects of her life that haven't already been recorded. Are there any stories she wants to tell? Most families have wonderful stories that bind them together. Is there anything she wants to write down? Is there anything she wants to capture on audio- or videotape for her children or future generations? There may be a variety of ways she would like to actively contribute to the legacy she leaves behind.

Also, ask if there is anything she needs you to complete or do for her, either before or after her death. There may be things she is worried about not accomplishing, like tending the vegetable or flower garden the way she always did, or making sure her daughter is taken shopping for a prom dress. It was very important to one woman I knew to orchestrate the purchasing of a gift for the awaited grandchild she was not going to live to see. The requests might be simple, such as giving a message to someone, or she may need your help in visiting, or contacting someone before she dies. You may be surprised by what she tells you, or even delighted. A woman I know had an Italian great-grandmother who wanted her to videotape a message from her to be played at the wake in case any fights broke out.

REMINISCING

One of the very important aspects of all goodbyes is paying attention to what we are saying goodbye to. This is particularly important in the case of death. So when someone is dying, saying goodbye is as much about life as it is about death.

Talk about what their life has been, and what they have contributed not only to you, but to society and their community. Listen as they talk about their memories. You will learn more about them, expanding the legacy they leave. Share with them memories you have about times spent together, or things about them that have always been meaningful to you. Often, with reminiscing, there is much laughter. And what greater tribute to a relationship than to know that you have brought each other joy!

Family picture albums, scrapbooks, and the mementos collected over the years are all wonderful aids to reminiscing. Moments looking at old pictures and recalling the stories that went along with them can give you memories that you will cherish. Ask them to tell you about other mementos around the house—old records, clothing, objects collected on vacation—the many things that will help recapture their past. Paying tribute to their life is largely what saying goodbye is all about.

Reminiscing can also give you an opportunity to address old conflicts that you have never talked about, but have always carried weight in your relationship. Take the opportunity to say, "Remember when—I never told you this, but I've always wanted to . . ." Sometimes this type of situation gives you an opening to say "I'm sorry," or to hear the same from the person who is dying. Again, working through old conflicts before someone dies can be tricky, but it can be done. Think carefully about whether you want to take the risk and try to resolve the problem, or let your last opportunity slip by. If you broach the subject sensitively and it seems like the conversation isn't getting anywhere constructive, you can always drop it. If you remain silent, you can't turn back the clock.

Remember that in Chapter Five, "Even Difficult Relationships Require Goodbyes," I give specific suggestions and examples for how to approach saying goodbye in especially difficult relationships.

TALK ABOUT LIFE

Sometimes, when someone is dying, they are determined to avoid all discussion of death. They may be too caught up in anger, so determined not to die, or so fearful of their own feelings that they won't get near them themselves, let alone allow you or anyone else near these tender feelings. If you have tried communicating your own feelings openly and were turned down, and if you have given clear invitations to talk and these have been rejected, you can still have a satisfying goodbye.

If you can't talk about death when saying goodbye, focus your energy on talking about their life. You can reminisce about times you've shared together, and ask them about aspects of their life that you don't know about. You can tell them how you feel with statements like:

- "Seeing you so sick makes me stop and think about how much you mean to me."
- "I remember how much fun we had on that trip to . . ."
- "I'll never forget how close I felt to you when . . ."
- "You were so good to me during that time when . . ."
- "I think sometimes I've forgotten to tell you how special you are to me."
- "Do you have the energy now to tell me any stories or favorite memories from when you were young?"

You can be honest and tell them what you need to without using the word "death." The result, in many ways, will be the same. You will be able to look back and know that they heard from you the importance they hold for you. You will have given them the opportunity to share what *they* wanted to be known and remembered about their life.

Two

Planning Ahead

Do what you can, with what you have, where you are.
—TEDDY ROOSEVELT

A very important part of supporting a person who is dying, and of saying goodbye, is being able to talk about his impending death, and all the decisions and choices that need to be made about his medical care. In our world of advanced medical technology, we need to be able to talk about death *before* we are confronted with life-threatening situations. You may well find yourself in the position of needing to make life-or-death choices for a person you love—a task that is much more manageable when you've discussed, in some detail, what they would have wanted.

I've seen problems arise so many times when families haven't talked openly about the preferences of a dying person. Then the time comes when they are forced to make life-and-death decisions, and the person who is dying is no longer in a position where he can speak for himself. Different family members have different ideas about what he would have wanted. Who is right? Who decides?

This is a terrible time to be paralyzed with uncertainty. You not only have to face the death of a person you care deeply about, but you risk losing one of the aspects that can be comforting—knowing you are helping the person you love get the care he or she would have wanted.

People are hesitant to even mention the possibility of death, for fear it will rob the sick person of hope if he knows that others around him are planning for his death. Keep in mind that there is always hope—hope for many different things. What you or the dying person specifically hope for may change moment to moment, depending on what is happening medically, or what mood people are in. Sometimes you hope for a cure. Or, as the person gets sicker, your hope might shift to holding on for a few more days or weeks to make it to an important event, such as a wedding or a birth. Hope for different things— even things that seemingly conflict often sits side by side.

If a person you care about is sick enough that they need you to advocate for them, talk with them about what they value, and want for themselves. Your invitation and encouragement to talk need not rob them of hope. You are merely joining with them to help them get what they want.

Talking is crucial, but so is having current information that will help guide your discussions about decisions near the end of life. This chapter outlines two important areas you will need to discuss with the person you love about how he wants decisions made on his behalf. The section on advance directives includes a description of the legal documents he can fill out that give you guidelines for the kind of treatment decisions he wants made for him—when to focus on curative or life-prolonging treatments, and when to focus on comfort measures.

This chapter also covers options for care: choosing the place for the final stage of life.

Life Needs Planning

In the past, when we had life-threatening or terminal illnesses, nature took its course and we generally died quickly. Now modern medicine has developed many ways to keep us alive longer, to treat or cure illnesses we used to die of. We have machines to keep us breathing or take over for our kidneys, we can replace organs when they stop working, and we can deliver fluids and nutrition through tubes into the stomach, or directly into the bloodstream.

Along with all the obvious benefits of medical advancement have come a series of new challenges. Now we have more choices, and the responsibility for making good choices. This means you need to be prepared to make choices about what you *do* want done for, and to you, when you are ill and, also, what you *do not* want done when you are too ill to receive benefit from a treatment.

Who decides the definition of "benefit," or when the cost outweighs the benefit? There is much gray area in this domain. What is appropriate? What are "extraordinary" or "heroic" measures in the event of catastrophic illness? The answers to these questions are very personal, and depend on your values, religious or spiritual beliefs, and the specific medical condition of the dying person. As in most areas having to do with life and death, there are no rights and wrongs.

It can be heartrending to talk with someone who is sick about what he would like done for him if he is too ill to make decisions for himself. You may feel superstitious, as though talking about it will somehow jinx the situation, and increase the likelihood that the "worst-case scenario" you have discussed will happen. Like children who engage in magical thinking, and believe they can make things happen with their thoughts, we avoid the topic, as if we have the power to control death.

Keep this thought in mind—death is not really what needs to be talked about. Death will happen whether you talk about it or not, plan for it or not. It is *life* that needs planning. What everyone desperately needs to talk about is what we want for our life when we are very ill. How would *you* decide what you would or wouldn't want done for you, or to you, if you were in a condition where there was reasonable certainty that you would never regain bodily functions you lost, or that you would never regain a better level of health?

If death were the certain outcome from your condition, how would you want to live your final days or months? Under what conditions would you want your life extended by intervention, and when would you want comfort to be the sole focus? And, important, do you know how the people you love would answer these questions?

Many of us make general statements about our wishes, but few of us stop and think about how lacking these statements prove to be if we haven't thought them out, and discussed them in some detail. Statements like "I don't want to be kept alive on machines," "Pull the plug if I'm a vegetable," or "I don't believe in doing anything to hasten or cause death," will give guidance to some situations, but not in many others.

Most of us will need to make life-and-death decisions at

some point in our lives. Are you equipped for that eventuality? Sometimes you will need to make a choice about discontinuing life supports, such as a ventilator that keeps the person breathing. Sometimes the choice is about whether to discontinue food and fluids when the dying person is no longer able to eat or drink on his own. This same choice about whether to discontinue food and fluids may also come up when he is in the terminal phase of his illness, and would prefer that his body shut down more quickly, rather than losing all functioning in a very gradual and prolonged manner.

Or you may need to make one or more decisions about beginning a treatment that is of questionable value, but the only hope for prolonging his life, such as a respirator, kidney dialysis, or even the use of various medications. If the treatment brings with it the high likelihood of distressing or disabling side effects that might outweigh the possible benefits, your choices can be very difficult.

What Kinds of Questions Do You Need to Ask?

It is not possible to anticipate all the situations that may come up for you. But if you have talked with the dying person about what she would want in a variety of possible situations, and what she would like decisions based on, you will have very helpful guidelines for making decisions on her behalf. At a point when death—including psychological death, such as with severe dementia—is the inevitable outcome of her condition, how much intervention does she want to keep her body going when she has lost the ability to maintain any semblance of normal functioning?

Do you and the other people who may be involved in decision-making know what the person you love would want in certain circumstances? What does she hope you will do for her, in order to see she gets the best care available? Ask yourself if you know the answers to the following questions:

- What does she consider a natural death? Stopping all intervention when death is inevitable, continuing food and fluids, but not using a ventilator, or utilizing all available technology until her body gives out?
- What does she consider "heroic"? Cardiopulmonary resuscitation, the use of machinery, or all treatments, including fluids and antibiotics, once she is in the terminal stage of her illness?
- Does the dying person want as many days as modern medicine can grant him, regardless of his condition?
- Would he want to be on a machine to keep himself breathing when this would be necessary to sustain his life, but there is no reasonable expectation that his condition would improve? What defines a "reasonable expectation" in his mind?
- Would she want assistance with eating—nutrition and fluids delivered into her body through tubes—when she is no longer in a condition to swallow?
- When he is not going to get better, and will no longer be able to carry out basic functions on his own, does he want his body to follow a natural course, and have any further medical efforts directed only toward managing his distressing symptoms?
- Is there a time when she would want pain relief and

comfort to be the *only* goals for her care? If she is not given fluids, or is not using a ventilator, she may have fewer days or hours left, but her quality of life may be very different.

- Does he believe there is a difference between assisted suicide, and stopping the administration of fluids once a person is unable to swallow?
- What are the main things that give her life meaning?
- What abilities or attributes need to be intact for him to consider himself as "living"?

As in all other aspects of life, there are no right or wrong answers to these questions. The values, belief systems, and religious views of a person and their family are the determining factors in what is right and what is wrong in these situations. In order to be the best advocate, you need to have a clear understanding of how the dying person would make choices for himself.

Making Decisions at Difficult Times

There are many times when someone is very ill that he is *not* in a position to make decisions for himself. When you are facing the inevitable death of a person you love, the main source of comfort in this very difficult and painful situation is knowing that you are able to do for him what he would have wanted at a time when he is unable to fend for himself.

Making these decisions for someone you care deeply about without his input can be much harder than it seems it would be. If you end up in this position, you will be trying to make life-and-death decisions in the midst of great loss. You will probably need to draw on your intellect to make your best choices at a time when, emotionally, every fiber of your being is fighting against the fact that the person you love is dying. The difficulty may be compounded by lack of sensitivity from the medical staff, or pressure to make choices that are different from what you think the dying person would want. You might want treatment continued, believing that he would have wanted to fight for life up until the last possible moment, while the medical staff may be encouraging you to stop treatment on the grounds that it is futile.

Or you may find that you want to discontinue all life-prolonging (or suffering-prolonging) treatment, including feedings, and be told that it is unethical or illegal (a myth) to "starve a person to death." There is now legislation in all fifty states that recognizes the person's stated preferences, as long as they are clear, as the guide to treatment choices. "Advance Directives," discussed later in this chapter, can act as very practical tools for planning ahead. They can serve as a catalyst for end-of-life discussions with those you love, and also be your guide if you are in a situation where you need to make these decisions.

KATE

Kate's mother had lost consciousness following a stroke. She had been sick a lot over the past few years from poorly controlled diabetes and its complications, and now, after the stroke, it was not clear how much physical and mental function she would regain. Her kidneys were failing, and her doctor recommended starting dialysis. When Kate expressed reservations, he said her mother would die without it. Kate was horribly torn. She wanted to do all she could to help her mother live, but it certainly wasn't clear what kind of "life" her mother would have anyway. What was clear was that her mother's body seemed to be giving out, with one serious problem after another.

Kate agonized about what to do. She remembered a conversation from long ago when her mother had said she would never want to be kept alive on machines. But that was the last conversation they ever had about the topic of death. It was very unlikely that her mother would regain much functioning following her stroke. She would probably be very impaired. She wouldn't, however, necessarily be on machines—the doctor thought the kidney problems may be temporary. Still, Kate was pretty sure that her mother would not want to live like that.

Kate's aunt Nan, her mother's only sister, thought differently. Nan stressed that her mother was a very religious woman, who appropriately valued life and would want to do everything possible to take care of the life that God had given her. Nan saw withholding available treatment as a form of euthanasia, which was strongly opposed by their church. Kate agreed that her mother was a very religious woman, but because of this, believed that her mother would probably see this serious decline as the end of her life, and God taking her home. Worse still, the decision needed to be made fairly quickly. If she took no action, her mother would die soon, but once dialysis started, Kate knew that stopping a treatment would be a more difficult choice for her than not starting it to begin with.

Kate desperately wanted to honor her mother by making the choice that her mother would have wanted, but no amount of tears, conversations with the nurse, her mother's priest, or conversations with her aunt helped her feel closer to this knowledge. What hadn't been said then, couldn't be gleaned now.

Advance Care Planning—Tools for Planning Ahead

Over the past few decades, there have been a number of legal cases that have established the standard of right to self-determination, and the right to appoint someone to speak on your behalf if you are too ill to do so. There have also been cases that have established standards for appropriate and acceptable medical practice. Many of the cases involving choices for care made on behalf of people who were unable to speak for themselves have been won because of wishes those people communicated prior to their loss of ability to advocate for themselves.

Based on these legal cases, it is now recommended practice and in your best interest to make your wishes known, in writing, when you are healthy. In 1991 the U.S. Congress passed the Patient Self-Determination Act. This federal law requires that all health-care facilities receiving Medicare and Medicaid funds inform patients of their right to complete advance directives.

An advance directive is, quite simply, the direction you have given in advance of people needing to make decisions for you. There are two types of legal advance directive documents—a living will and a health-care proxy (also called a durable power of attorney). One or the other of these is legally binding in all fifty states, so it is important to learn which one is in your state. The instructions that you give in writing are your best assurance that any care decisions made will be in keeping with your belief systems.

LIVING WILL

A living will is a document in which you state your preferences for your medical care in the event that you would not be able to communicate on your own. In this document you detail the kind of treatment you would and would not want under specific medical conditions.

A living will has a definite advantage, in that you are able to "speak for yourself" when you are unable to communicate. This same advantage, however, can also be a disadvantage—because you may not have accurately anticipated the situation you will be in. For example, you may have stated that you do not want to be put on a respirator if you are terminally ill and in a coma, but suppose you develop an infection that would require one temporarily, before the underlying illness required one. Would you still want it withheld? Keep in mind that what people want in a given situation may be different than what they *thought* they would want ahead of time. The situation may also arise where you had specified one thing, but given the reality of the situation you end up in, family members believe you would have wanted something different.

HEALTH-CARE PROXY

Health-care proxy is another term for a medical power of attorney. A health-care proxy specifies the person you appoint to make decisions for you should you not be able to make them on your own. This person, your health-care agent, can be anyone of your choosing. Most often the person chosen is a family member, but does not have to be. The person who you choose should be someone you have faith in, and someone you believe will be able to carry out your wishes, regardless of whether she agrees with the wishes or beliefs you hold. And, of course, this person must be willing to accept your requests.

Your spouse, for example, may not be the best person to have for your proxy *if* she would be unable to let you die when the time came, despite her prior understanding of your wishes, and her assurances that she would abide by them. Once you have designated a proxy, and are in a condition where you are unable to speak for yourself, the proxy has full authority to make decisions. The proxy can change his or her mind about prior decisions the two of you made. This may seem obvious, but in order for your health-care agent to work effectively for you, *you must first talk at some length with them* to let them know what your wishes are.

There are some specific advantages to health-care proxies over living wills. Health-care proxies offer much more flexibility, in that the person who will assume responsibility will have the freedom to make decisions about the actual problems and questions that arise. They are not restricted by what you anticipated ahead of time. This can be important, since the medical course of an illness often varies somewhat from what is expected. As in Kate's story, had she and her mother discussed how her mother defined "life" and "death," or what level of intervention she considered in keeping with her religious beliefs, Kate would have been able to apply those beliefs to the specific situations that arose.

So, providing you have good conversations and a clear understanding with your health-care agent about how you would like your choices made, there is a high likelihood that your preferences will be carried out, regardless of the specific situation or problem. You need to have the necessary conversations ahead of time, and go into enough detail to have the person be able to make end-of-life decisions for you, even if you end up in a situation neither of you has anticipated.

Talking About Advance Care Planning

The best time to have discussions about advance directives is before anyone is coping with a specific illness, and when our human vulnerability to death is more of an abstraction than a reality. However, if the person you care about is sick, and has not completed the legal documents recognized in your state, now is the time to do so.

Talk at length with the dying person about what they want. This is probably the most important thing you can do for someone as they are dying. Be their advocate, their companion, and their comfort; be willing to hear their fears and their wishes as they leave this world.

Many people have difficulty bringing up such a sensitive topic, fearing that they are being insensitive by focusing on death at a time when the dying person's energy is going into focusing on hope. This need not be the case. Remember that the conversation you need to have with the dying person is really about living life, not specifically about death.

Sometimes you have to wait for the course of the illness to reveal itself before you can make decisions. The terrain of any illness or disease is unknown, and, even with advance directives and other planning tools, you may need to do your planning as you go along. Allow for uncertainty, but set some markers for what to look for. Gather as much information as you can, at different times during the course of the illness. View the process of questioning and decision-making as fluid, and changing, just as the course of the illness.

Remember that knowing the person well makes all the difference. Depending on the dying person's ability to communicate you may be relying on a nod, or a look in the eye to reassure you that you are making the best decisions you can for him.

WAYS TO START THE CONVERSATION
You know your own communication style and the style of the person who is dying. Below are some suggestions of different ways to go about beginning the conversation. Use them to jog your thinking, or help you think of wording that is comfortable for you.

- "I want to make sure you always get the best care possible, or the type of care that you want, so there are a few things we should talk about . . ."
- "I've been wondering if there are things that you want me to know about your beliefs, or wishes that would help me be sure you get the care you want . . ."
- "Since none of us knows what the future will bring, there are some things that I think we should all talk about . . ."
- "If I'm ever in a position where I need to make some health-care decisions for you, I'll be able to take care of you best if I know what you want . . ."

RALPH AND LOUISE

Ralph and his mother, Louise, were able to talk about all aspects of her illness, including her death. His experience with his mother stood in stark contrast to the death of his father a number of years earlier, who he had not been able to talk with at all.

"One of the things about my mother's death was that she felt she had lived a full life before she developed Lou Gehrig's disease. With that disease, there was no doubt she was going to die. We also knew that her body would give out, but her mind would remain sharp."

Louise and Ralph talked about what it meant for there to be "no heroic measures." Louise then worked with a lawyer to prepare a very thorough advance directive. But Louise and Ralph both knew the advance directive would not necessarily cover all of the possibilities she might encounter as her disease advanced. Also, Louise couldn't anticipate in advance when she would be ready to die; when she would be willing to say no to any further measures to keep herself alive.

"Mother knew that something would happen to signal her that 'Okay, this is the last thing, this is where I choose to not have anything more done.' We prepared ourselves for an event, but didn't know when that event would happen, or what it would be. We thought it would be that she would stop taking nutrition—that would be a method she could use to die."

Ralph, his wife, Kathleen, and Louise knew from the beginning that, as her disease progressed, Louise would probably have difficulty eating, and would need a feeding tube inserted into her stomach through the wall of the abdomen. They understood from her doctor that her illness was likely to progress either from the top down or the bottom up. Louise's illness progressed from the top down, so when she developed serious difficulty with swallowing, she still had many other capabilities. Her quality of life with the feeding tube would still be significant, and the consequences of not having it were that she would probably die fairly quickly. She wasn't able to talk at that time, but she was fully involved in conversations and decisions about her treatment by typing on her laptop computer. She decided to have a feeding tube inserted.

Louise's nursing home arranged a meeting with her entire health-care team, including her physician, her nurse practitioner, and other nursing home staff, and health-care workers. They had her advance care directive on hand, and let the team know there would be some point when Louise didn't want any further lifesaving measures, and that they didn't know when that would be. They discussed that it might be ending her nutrition.

"During the meeting I knew I had to ask one of the hardest questions I've ever had to ask. 'What will happen when she stops taking the nutrition, and how long will it take?' Her doctor said she would get dehydrated, and we can make her comfortable during that time by putting wrapped-up ice cubes on her forehead and lips, and it will take between seven and ten days."

Four months later, Louise developed an infection surrounding the feeding tube, and after a conversation with the doctor, she chose this event as the one she would not go beyond. By then she was unable to speak, or to use her laptop computer, but with Ralph, Kathleen, and her doctor present, Louise made her wishes known by shaking her head no.

"I think, just as the doctor said, it took eight days, and Kathleen and I spent a lot of time with ice cubes. On the morning of the eighth day, she had her nurse call us to ask to make certain we came that day, and that was the day she died. We got there in the morning, and let her know we were ready for her to leave if she was, and she responded to that—I could see the response in her eyes. About six hours later, she did leave. She wanted to do it well for her, for us, and for other people to learn by."

Start the conversation any way you can. The unspoken usually carries more weight than that which is spoken. If you begin the discussion with some knowledge of where you want to come out, and what you need to cover, and you go slowly and listen to each other, you will do fine. Letting fears be your guide often leads to regret. This lesson applies to all of life, not only the end-of-life discussion this chapter is focused on.

Talking can create closeness. Talking with the person you love about matters as emotionally stirring as sickness and death gives you an extraordinary opportunity to share, support one another, and increase closeness—a true gift at the end of life, or anytime.

Preferences on CPR

When the dying person's illness is far progressed, one of the choices you might be asked to make is whether or not to forgo cardiopulmonary resuscitation should his heart stop beating. This instruction, a DNR (Do Not Resuscitate), is signed when the illness is so far progressed that little will be gained from re-suscitation efforts—either medical personnel will most likely fail to revive the person, or they will revive him, but he will likely only live for a few more hours or days.

This choice should be discussed with your doctor. If the dying person is very ill, and they are at a point where they're ready to stop fighting the illness and gear all efforts toward comfort and quality of life, ask your doctor, if he or she has not already raised the issue, to talk with you and the dying person about this option. Take the initiative—do not assume that your doctor will broach the topic if not pushed to do so.

Once a DNR has been signed, keep it in an obvious spot, such as on the refrigerator, if the dying person is at home. If they are in the hospital or another health-care facility, make sure there is a copy in their chart, and that all of the personnel involved in their care are aware of this instruction. Unfortunately, you can't assume that having signed the form, and knowing it is in the medical record, is enough to be sure that the medical staff knows your wishes and directives. In addition to the written form, be sure to *tell them.*

Options for Care—Choosing the Place for the Final Stage of Life

While the majority of people in the United States still die in the hospital, in recent years this trend has been changing. Due to a variety of factors—insurance changes, shorter hospital stays, the growth of the hospice movement, and more recently, money going into medical and public education regarding options and choices in care of the dying, more and more people are dying in settings other than the hospital. There are a growing number of programs that offer care—at home and in facilities—providing more holistic care for people with life-threatening illnesses. Know what your options are, so you can make your best choice.

HOSPICE

Hospice is a program of care for people who have terminal illnesses, have completed curative or life-prolonging treatments, and are at a point where they choose to have care geared toward maintaining comfort, controlling pain and other distressing symptoms, and maximizing quality of life. Hospice is generally a philosophy of care, not necessarily a place where care is provided. Although there are some residential units, most hospice care is delivered in people's homes or in the long-term care facility where they live. Hospice care provides a multidisciplinary team that can address the issues involved in end-of-life care, including medical care, pain and symptom management, and emotional and spiritual care.

The different team members: generally, a nurse, social worker, chaplain, and home health aid will come to the home or nursing home, wherever the sick person is living, to work, along with the family, to meet the needs of that person. Hospice also uses volunteers who stay with dying people for companionship when they are alone, to be there in case of emergency, or to help give the family a break. To qualify for hospice services, a person must have a terminal illness, have ended all curative or life-prolonging treatments, and be, to the best of their doctor's knowledge, in their last six months of life.

PALLIATIVE CARE

Palliative care programs are similar to hospice, in that they are for people with life-threatening or life-limiting illnesses that don't respond to curative treatment. Palliative care also provides a team approach to meeting physical, psychological, and spiritual needs, and is geared toward comfort and quality of life rather than cure. They can provide care either in a person's home or in an inpatient setting.

There are a few differences between hospice and palliative care programs. Palliative care does not have the limitation of requiring that all curative or life-prolonging treatments have ended, nor does the person have to be within the last six months of life. This is particularly important in illnesses that have a less predictable course—heart disease, lung disease, Alzheimer's, AIDS, or amyotrophic lateral sclerosis (ALS), otherwise known as Lou Gehrig's disease. The palliative care team can work collaboratively to address end-of-life concerns with your oncologist, cardiologist, or other specialist. Palliative care is, however, relatively new and not as well defined as hospice. There is much more variation from place to place in the makeup of the multidisciplinary team. Unlike hospice there is no specific insurance benefit for coverage of palliative care multidisciplinary services; some of the services ideally offered by a palliative care team may not be covered by many insurance policies.

HOME CARE PROGRAMS

Visiting Nurse Associations (VNAs) provide home care for all kinds of illnesses—both short term and long term. There are restrictions on care, however, such as the Medicare requirement that a person be homebound in order to receive care. Community nursing agencies vary in their focus on caring for the dying. All VNAs care for people at the end of life and at the time of death, but for many of them caring for the dying is a relatively small amount of the work they do. Expertise in pain and symptom management, as well as comfort in addressing the social, emotional, and spiritual aspects of dying, may or may not be their forte.

LONG-TERM CARE FACILITY

Many people have a negative reaction to the idea of a nursing home or chronic care facility, and want to care for the dying person at home. However, despite all good intentions, there are instances when very sick people are not safe at home, or when the round-the-clock medical or physical demands exceed the abilities of home resources. In these cases, it may be best for the dying person to be in a facility that is staffed twenty-four hours a day, leaving more time and energy for family and friends to provide the emotional support that is so important at this time.

Making Realistic Care Choices

When you are considering options for care, it's important to talk about the wishes or desires of all involved parties, and the realities of who will and won't be able to do what. Get as much information as possible. What can you expect over the course of their illness? What are the probabilities and the realistic possibilities? What kind of physical care is the dying person likely to need?

Ask the dying person's doctor very specific questions about their illness and its expected course. While no one can say exactly what's going to happen in the future, most illnesses have some predictability in their course, even though the doctor probably will not know how long the process will take, or what the individual course will be exactly. Ask your doctor the following questions:

- What, specifically, should we expect?
- What are the typical problems that arise with this illness?
- What should we watch for?
- Are there symptoms we should be particularly concerned about?

- What support services would you expect us to need?
- Who should we talk to for comprehensive information on services available to help us with his care?

Given what you are told, look at the reality of the situation, and ask yourself the following questions:

- Who is in the household, and how available are they?
- Are there people who will be able to spell each other, so everyone will be able to get to sleep?
- What is the health and stamina of the person who is going to take the primary responsibility for care?
- What is the emotional temperament of the person who will be giving the bulk of the care?

Oftentimes, people desperately *want* to take care of the person they love when they are dying, but the burdens of care are, quite simply, too great. Even when things go smoothly, caring for someone who is dying is extremely demanding. Nothing is more devastating than feeling like you failed to give a person you love good care at such a critical time. Because of this, it is important to make informed and careful choices—not just based on what you *want* to do for the person who is dying, but on what is realistic as well.

Family Involvement

Family members may have very different ideas about what they, or others in the family should do, what is in whose best interest, and how particular goals can best be accomplished.

As early as possible in the illness of a family member, hold a family meeting. If your family is one where conflict is high, or one that generally has difficulty communicating and coming to agreements, it may work best for everyone if you ask a professional therapist or social worker to facilitate the meeting. If views were always very divergent in your family, don't expect unanimous agreement now. Work toward compromise.

The same holds true if you and your family agree, and simply want to say what needs to be said, but you feel afraid that you will lose your way in the conversation because of the intensity of feelings. In these situations it can be very helpful to have a knowledgeable "guide" that is not a family member.

GUIDELINES FOR THE MEETING

Stay focused on the problem at hand, the present management and future planning around the illness of the sick person, and their end-of-life issues. If you have had a lot of conflict in your family in the past, don't try to hash through old disagreements at this point. Start with information gathering (often people are working on erroneous assumptions about what everyone else is thinking and feeling), and ask each other the following questions:

- What is your understanding of the current situation and the prognosis?
- What are your main concerns or fears?
- What is your understanding of the dying person's wishes, in regards to their illness and medical treatment?
- What matters most to you?

- What matters least?
- What do we all expect of each other, and what assumptions are being made about who will do what?

At the end of the meeting, review what was said—are there/were there any misunderstandings that can be cleared up? If it hasn't already been done, appoint a person or persons who will take the primary responsibility for coordinating care and communication.

Planning the Remembrances

Although we shy away from talking with people about life going on after their death, many people like the opportunity to actively participate in some way in the legacy they are leaving. The rituals around death are one of the ways you can focus on that person's legacy. Dying people have often lost much of their ability to care not only for themselves, but also, for the people they love. Oftentimes, they are grateful for the opportunity to participate in something they believe will help make things easier for those who they love and are leaving behind. Choosing music they love, or readings that capture what they want expressed once they are not there, gives them an opportunity to state who they are, and this can feel very important.

However, this is not for everyone. One woman I know took great joy in carefully planning all the details of her funeral with her daughter—the flowers, a poem, the music, and a letter she had written expressing her appreciation to all those who enriched her life, Still another woman who was dying felt very differently. Her son kept pushing her to talk about what she wanted for her memorial service, and other details, such as the place to scatter her ashes. "I know I'm going to die soon," she told me, "but, frankly, I really don't like thinking much about everybody's life going on once I'm gone. It won't matter much to me then. I guess they can do whatever they like that makes them feel good."

As in all other areas when dealing with the end of life, there is not a right or wrong, but it is important to have the choice. Extend the invitation to talk, express your wishes if you would like to, and listen carefully to what you are told. If she shows interest in joining or taking the lead in the plans, welcome it, talk with her, and listen. If she pulls back from the idea, don't push it, believing it is in her best interest to participate. Respect her wishes, and make your own plans accordingly.

Taking Care of Yourself

Get support—emotional and physical—for yourself. When someone in your life is very sick, unless you are in the medical profession, you are immediately thrust into a new world. The pressure to know everything you can know medically about their situation, to comfort and protect them as they enter this new, frightening world, and to manage your own fears and daily life can easily feel overwhelming. You will need to pay particular attention to asking for help from friends, family, and professionals.

You may also want to consider joining one of many support groups that exist for family and friends of dying people. Sometimes they are specific to a particular kind of disease or illness, such as cancer or ALS. These groups can be an invaluable place to share information when going through the experience, and about planning ahead.

Finally, talk with someone about what you want when you are near death. Talking about what you want as death nears can become easier as you go along—but you need to start somewhere. Most of us learn how to talk in many difficult and fearful situations in our lives—in difficult relationships, through divorces, job loss, and other losses. But, because we only die once, we do not get much practice talking about what we or the people we love want as we near death.

Once you do begin talking about what you want at the last stage of life, you will likely find that it is a fulfilling and gratifying experience. One that allows you to share what you have found most important in your life, and for that reason, brings you closer to those you love.

THREE

The Dying Process

Honest listening is one of the best medicines
we can offer the dying and the bereaved.
—JEAN CAMERON (DYING OF CANCER IN 1982)

The way people approach dying is as varied as the ways in which they approach living, since dying is, of course, part of life. In all aspects of the life cycle—from childhood through the intimate relationships we have in our adult years, and into old age—our overall personalities stay much the same in some very basic ways, but also develop and change as we gain life experience.

If you tend to be quiet and introspective, perhaps you grow a little and more openly share yourself over time, but you will probably be on the quiet side all of your life. If you are outgoing and demonstrative, you may become more introspective with life's experiences, but will probably remain primarily outgoing. Or, equally as possible, if you grew up angry and afraid, depending on your reaction to life experiences, you could become even more angry and afraid in middle and old age. We like to think we will become "mellow" with age, but coping with the losses of aging—sickness and death being two of the most certain ones—is difficult, and if we've had a tough time dealing with adversity earlier in life, it won't automatically get better as we get older!

No matter what the dying person's personality is like, some common psychological and physical elements that most deaths share are: fear and uncertainty about what is to come; a sense of aloneness; and a need for companionship and comfort—both physical and emotional. There are no sure recipes for what to say to, or do for, a person near death, but if you enter the picture prepared for what her needs are likely to be, and a willingness to communicate with her throughout the experience, you will have a good start.

The unfortunate phrase "There's nothing you can do" comes from the framework that death is the ultimate failure. If you can't cure or postpone, you have nothing of value to offer. The fact is, there are *always* things you can do—especially if you shift your focus from curing to caring and comfort. Again, there are *always* things you can do to help someone remain comfortable in their final days of life, both physically and emotionally. You can offer them the valuable and simple gifts of your touch, or your presence. The most important thing you can do is let the dying person know you are available.

The Right Way to Die

There is no one "right" way to die any more than there is any one "right" way to live. While this may sound obvious, I don't think we put this idea into practice all that often. The longer I'm in this field, first as a nurse and now as a psychologist, caring for the dying and their families, the more I think that we, as a society, have very high and unrealistic expectations of the dying. If people with life-threatening illnesses are expressing too much distress or despair, we are quick to label them depressed, hopeless, or as not being in the "right" frame of mind to fight the illness. But when they are expressing primarily hope and determination, they're accused of being "in denial," as if lack of despair is a sign of some sort of psychological shortcoming.

An eighty-three-year-old woman I know, Dolores, who has had a lifelong attitude that *No hardship is too great to bear or learn from*, is approaching the losses of old age with this same attitude, one that I'm sure she will carry with her till the moment she dies. Dolores has experienced more than her share of difficult circumstances in life: One of her children was born with retardation, two of her children died before the age of twenty, her husband died early in life, and a subsequent late-in-life marriage failed. Yet Dolores thrives on meeting even the worst disappointments with humor, and a renewed investment in life. In anticipating her own death and funeral, she called the local mortician and asked why she simply couldn't be buried in her backyard under the maple tree. After all, she would be donating her organs to medical science, why not just put what is left out in the back, like the family dog?

Now, as Dolores grows older and more frail—she is quickly losing her sight and her hearing—I sometimes get concerned that this seemingly easy attitude about death is really bravado, and she is frightened and suffering without anyone to confide in. But this is me, not Dolores. When I make myself step back and really think about Dolores's way of going about life, I believe she isn't afraid. She has many people who care about her, and she talks with any of them as much as she wants and needs to. It is me, not her, who is afraid for her. It can be so easy to assume, without even thinking about it, that others must, on some level, feel the same way we do.

When I keep my own assumptions in check, I can be there for Dolores in ways that fit with who she is, and in those ways I can offer her support and comfort. Dolores, unlike me, would not feel comfortable talking directly about her fears. But she does like to recount family stories, and get calls and letters, and when I visit, she relishes my companionship, and my help with the daily tasks of living that have become increasingly more difficult for her.

What we need to be aware of, and sensitive to, is that each dying person finds his or her own way to make sense of, and cope with, all that is happening. Only when we can meet them where they are, do we have something to offer.

We Each Have Our Own Way of Dying—Martha

Martha was thirty-two when she was fighting the last stage of breast cancer. Over the time that she fought the disease, through radiation, surgery, and chemotherapy, she was never willing to entertain the idea that she would die. She told friends there was no way this disease was going to "get her." She saw a nutritionist, an herbalist, and a psychic. She meditated, tried visualization, read about alternative treatment modalities, and sought second and third opinions from oncologists. She tried every chemotherapy suggested to her, despite the horrendous side effects. She got thinner, weaker, and sicker, sometimes from the illness and other times from the treatment itself.

Her friends were worried about her. They'd talk among themselves about their concern that Martha was "not facing the reality of her illness." They worried that she was in denial, and that at some point the reality of her disease and her poor response to treatment would hit her hard. Each of her friends tried talking to her in their own way. Martha met any suggestion that she might die from this illness with irritation, or icy silence.

The last time Martha went into the hospital she had high fevers, and despite numerous tests, her doctors could not find a source. She received antibiotics, blood transfusions, and intravenous nutrition. Each time something was suggested that might possibly help, she chose to try it. Sometimes her friends were furious at the entire medical world for holding out hope that seemed in vain. They wanted their friend to be at peace. They took turns sitting with her, sponged her when her fever was high, and massaged lotion into her thin skin. They put her brightly colored get well cards up all over her walls, and kept her favorite music playing throughout the day. Never once, up through her last breath, did Martha ever admit that she was dying.

Reflecting on Martha's death six months after she died, Jillian, Martha's best friend, described how differently she now thought about the experience. "You know," she said, "it seems now that things went the way they should. Martha was always a fighter; she was determined to work her hardest to make things go the way she wanted. She was so fiery and pigheaded, and those were some of the things we all loved about her.

"I like remembering her that way. So I guess she was right all along, her disease never did get the better of her."

Martha didn't want to think, let alone talk, about anything other than getting better, but in case she did—Jillian and her other friends all knew they had given her the chance to. They remained available to Martha throughout her illness, even though it was not her way to talk with them specifically about her death. They gave her many invitations to talk about her fears and concerns. Each time, she let them know she was not approaching her illness in this way. We each have our own way of dying, and of dealing with another's death.

They respected her wishes, and found other ways to support themselves, and their own discomfort over Martha's way of dealing with her illness. Martha made her choices and called the shots up until the end—just as she always had.

Especially if the dying person's way of coping is very different from your own, it is important for *you* to find the support you need. If she rejects your invitations to talk, or your concerns, find other people with whom you can share your experiences. In Martha's case, her friends were able to talk with each other at length about their feelings as they faced Martha's impending death. They offered each other a community of support during a time when it was desperately needed.

Being with another person as they approach death inevitably brings up thoughts and feelings about your own death. How will it be for me? Will I do it well? What do I think well is? You won't truly know until your time comes how you will handle your own death, but when these feelings and questions are triggered by someone else's death, it is a good time to begin exploring them. Seek out someone you trust to explore your feelings with.

Emotional Changes Near Death

While it's true that for the most part the people you love will be who they have always been as they approach death, you will see some emotional changes as they get closer to their final days. Exactly what you see will be a result of how they confront the constantly changing challenges and demands of their illness. As they meet those demands, they will be experiencing new sides of themselves that will be new to you, too. And you too will undergo your own changes from the demands the death puts upon you.

FEAR, ESPECIALLY OF BEING ALONE

Some of the most difficult emotional aspects of approaching death—for both dying people and their caregivers—have to do with the feelings and fears of being alone. Those who are dying often fear being left alone as they become more debilitated and dependent, and as others around them pull away due to the emotional distress they feel because of the impending death of someone they love.

Caregivers feel alone too as they manage the day-to-day care of the dying person, and struggle with the many difficult feelings they have as they watch someone they love suffer. The demands of taking care of a seriously ill person are enormous. When caregivers are immersed in this all-consuming world, they often feel like they are the only ones going through this sort of experience. They also live with the sadness that when death comes, they will be left alone without the person they love.

This fear of being left alone is one of the greatest fears encountered by many. It is also, in many ways, the most manageable. Look at the following suggestions—for both caregivers and the person who is ill—for countering the fear and anxiety of being alone:

- To give comfort to the dying person—join with him. You can do this by talking with him, doing things for him, and, perhaps most important, sitting with him quietly. By staying at his side, you let him know he is not alone; that you won't leave him emotionally in the last stretch of his life. This is one of the greatest gifts you can give.

- For yourself if you are the caregiver—find time to talk with others about your own experience. Here it's probably more accurate to say *make* the time—if you are a primary caregiver, free time doesn't exist. Talk to other people who have been caregivers to someone who is dying, whether they're friends, colleagues at work, a caregiver support group, or other family members. It's amazing how comforting it can be just to know that you are not the only person experiencing this.

ANXIETY AND/OR DEPRESSION

The anxiety that people feel when facing death tends to have three basic sources. The first is the aspect of not knowing what is going to happen to them in the course of their illness. People worry: Will I be in pain? Will my body betray me in ways I can't manage? You can counter this kind of anxiety by getting good information about the expected course of the disease—what are the likely symptoms?—and knowing what drugs or other treatments will be available to manage pain.

The second source of anxiety, sadness, or depression is often about the loss of a future in which they will not participate. It is very difficult for many people to look ahead and know they will not be around to share in marriages, births, the growth of grandchildren, and other important life events. It can be very hard for a dying mother, for example, to look at her young children and know they will go through the pain of losing a mother so early on in their lives. Acknowledge to the dying person that you understand she might be concerned about the future, and let her know you would like to hear what she thinks, worries, or feels about this. Having you available to listen to these feelings will not take away all of the feelings, but it will probably help diminish their intensity. If nothing else, she will no longer be alone as she grapples with these difficult feelings.

The third source of anxiousness has to do with a general anxiety about death, which couples with the fear of being alone. We all have a basic death anxiety. Death is an unknown, and an end to what we do know—life. Ultimately, we each face death alone. Others may escort us right up to the last moment, but we go to death alone. This existential anxiety that dying people feel can be exacerbated by fears that they will be left, even before their death, by those they care about.

DIFFICULTY WITH INCREASING DEPENDENCE
Most adults have a hard time giving up, or losing, the level of independence they have achieved. It is hard to lose control over aspects of our lives and our bodies that we have grown to take for granted. As adults, we don't like having to depend on others for feeding or basic hygiene. As people get sicker, they experience many milestones of not being able to do something they were once able to do. They may go from being able to walk, to being in a wheelchair, or being able to go to the bathroom by themselves, to needing a bedpan. Or they may need

to give up driving, or move in with other family members who can care for them. These kinds of losses can seem like mini-deaths; a new loss to grieve along the way.

If the dying person expresses frustration at these losses, try the following:

- Listen to them, imagine yourself in their shoes, and empathize.
- Don't try to convince them that this isn't as bad as it seems.
- Help them maintain the maximum amount of independence and control they are able to manage. After listening, think through with them the aspects of a task they *are* able to do, and encourage them to do all they realistically can.

QUESTIONS ABOUT THE MEANING OF THEIR LIFE

Dying people often spend far more of their time looking back rather than forward. Death is an unknown, and to many people, depending on their religious or spiritual beliefs, there aren't a lot of specifics to think about (other than wondering about death). The life they have lived, however, does have many specifics, and this is what most people spend their time thinking about as they near the end of their life—the many details that comprised it.

Hope is an extremely important aspect of our existence. The process of living with a terminal illness usually involves the redefinition of "hope." Rarely do dying people lose all hope, but *what* they hope for changes—a cure, a few more months, the chance to still be alive for an anticipated event, to be without pain, to die peacefully, to help ease the pain of loved ones they're leaving behind. What, exactly, a person hopes for is very personal. Ask her what she hopes for in the present, and in her time remaining. Don't assume she doesn't have hope, simply because she is dying. Ask the following questions to offer comfort or assistance:

- Is there anyone you want to see, or communicate with that you haven't gotten a chance to?
    - You may want to sit with her and reminisce about family and friends. This can help her remember who she has shared good times with, and felt close to, and may want to let know she is dying.
    - Offer to make phone calls, or otherwise contact people she might want to see, or talk with.
    - You may also offer to help entertain any visitors she wishes to see. In this way you can lighten the mood of a gathering, and also reassure her that when she is tired of visiting, you will take charge and help usher the visitors out the door.
- Is there anything you especially want to do in the time you have left?
- Are there ways you want to be remembered? Do you want to talk about that now, or in the future?
    - Some people want to document their life or offer something to descendents in writing, or on a video- or audiotape.
    - Some people want to help plan their funeral or memorial service, choosing readings and music that express aspects of themselves they want remembered.

- One man and his mother, together, wrote her obituary. Writing was an interest they had always shared, and it gave them a wonderful opportunity to talk about her life, and what she wanted to be remembered for.

• Is there anything you would like me, or someone else, to do for you, or in your memory, in the future?

- One woman who had been very involved in the arts left a small scholarship of a few hundred dollars a year to her community arts organization. Each year the scholarship is awarded to the most promising beginning artist, and one of the judges is her son.
- A man who was devoted to gardening, and took great pride in the beauty of his front yard garden, asked that his neighbors maintain his garden after he was gone.

Physical Changes Near Death

One of the most difficult things for caregivers, and for the dying person, can be the overall physical decline before death. Knowing generally what to expect, and preparing physically and emotionally for these changes, can make a big difference in how comfortable—again, physically and emotionally—everyone involved in the process feels.

DECREASED ENERGY

As dying people get sicker, they are likely to reevaluate how they want to use their time and energy. They tire much more quickly, and can no longer do what they were able to do in the past. There is a fine line between encouraging someone to get out and do something pleasurable to help enrich his daily experiences, or improve his overall mood, and *pushing* him to do things he is not really up to doing. Use some of the following guidelines for how to navigate this area:

- Talk to the dying person. "How are you feeling today?" "What is your energy level?" Listen carefully to what he is telling you he needs, and why.
- Encourage him to pay attention to the messages he is getting from his body. "How does your breathing feel today?" "Do you still have that weakness in your hands?" "Any more of that dizziness you talked about yesterday?"
- Support him in making his choices carefully, and setting realistic goals. This involves helping him sort out whether a given task or activity is something he would *like* to do or is trying to do because he thinks he *should*. If he's engaging in activity because he thinks he should, help him stop and think through whether this is necessary.
  - Is there someone you/we can delegate the task to?
  - What will you lose by handing the task off to someone else, or letting it go undone?
- If, on the other hand, he truly would like to do the activity, help him think through what will make it doable.
  - What amount of physical energy will the task require? How much time?

- If the physical demands are too great, is there a way to break the task or activity down into more manageable parts?
- Avoid the temptation to encourage him to push himself, thinking that this will help him fight the illness.

DECREASED APPETITE

Feeding someone is very often equated with nurturing and love. It can be very difficult to see a person we love stop eating. We often feel like we are not taking good care of him or her. However, forcing someone to eat when she doesn't want to, encouraging her to eat more than her body is telling her she needs, or trying to get her to eat different types of food than what she wants will only increase her discomfort. Remember that the weight loss you see in a dying person may be due, in large part, to the disease process, not just due to lack of nutrition. Watching a dying person's appetite decline can stir up feelings of helplessness in both the dying person and in any caregivers, but there are ways that you can help. The following suggestions might help ease the discomfort of the person who is sick:

- Encourage her to eat smaller portions more frequently. Smaller meals are easier to eat than three large meals.
- If she is nauseous, try cool or cold foods—they often go down more easily than hot foods.
- Try bland foods and soft foods, such as puddings and ice cream—they may be more appealing.
- Drinks, such as frappes, malts or sodas, may go down well. (Don't, however, force fluids. This can result in

fluid retention, swelling, respiratory congestion, or bed-wetting.)

FOR NAUSEA, THE FOLLOWING MIGHT ALSO BE HELPFUL:

- Help her with good mouth care. If she doesn't have the strength or muscle control to brush her teeth, offer to help her. If her gums have sores or are too sensitive for brushing, you can clean her mouth by gently swabbing the surface of her tongue and gums with large cotton swabs soaked in cool water, or commercially prepared ones soaked in sugar water. Pay special attention to the areas where secretions collect, such as between the gums and cheeks.
- Have hard candies, lollipops, or ice chips on hand. Sucking on these will help keep the mucous membranes moist, and will add to her comfort.
- Keep household odors to a minimum. Normal smells from the kitchen may become difficult for her to tolerate. Carefully choose what you cook, and ventilate the room well.
- Medication is often helpful for nausea—check with her doctor.

SHORTNESS OF BREATH/DIFFICULTY BREATHING

Whether due to the disease process, treatment side effects, weakness, or other causes, many people have difficulty breathing at some point in later stages of their illness. Most people find shortness of breath a very difficult symptom to tolerate, and it tends to escalate anxiety fairly quickly. It also causes a high degree of ongoing distress. If he is having trouble breathing, be sure to speak with your doctor or nurse about this symptom. He may need to be put on oxygen.

Try the following to help a sick person breathe more comfortably:

- Elevate the head of the bed. Breathing is generally easier in this position because gravity is working with the person, not against him—his abdominal organs aren't pressing against his diaphragm, leaving less room for his lungs.
- Keep the room a comfortable temperature, perhaps on the cool side, and keep the air circulating, either with an open window, or a fan that is not pointing directly at him. A warm room with still air makes breathing feel more difficult.
- Communicate using a gentle approach; speak quietly and calmly.
- Help him practice relaxation techniques, such as muscle relaxation, visualization, or meditation. Or try distraction techniques, such as reading to him, playing music, or putting on a movie. Anything that you know will help reduce his anxiety level will also be helpful in treating his shortness of breath.

CONSTIPATION OR DIARRHEA

With many illnesses, people tend to have problems keeping their bowel patterns regular. Compared to the topic of death, the bowels may not seem very important. However, no one can be comfortable and relaxed when they are suffering from constipation or frequent diarrhea. Both may be due to the disease process or a side effect of various treatments. Constipation can cause pain or a feeling of fullness, and exacerbate problems with appetite or breathing. Diarrhea will increase weakness, cause electrolyte imbalances, increase weight loss, and can exacerbate emotional distress, especially if the dying person has any episodes of incontinence.

People often find it embarrassing to talk about their bowel movements, and you will probably do best to ask directly, "Are you having any problems with your bowels?" Straightforward questions do more to suggest that this is an important and acceptable thing to talk about than do questions that try to "delicately" approach the topic. Talk with his doctor or nurse about appropriate treatment. He may need to have his diet altered, medication, or some other treatment. Also, make sure he can get to the bathroom easily, and that there is a commode by his bed.

Pain Management

Pain is a symptom of many illnesses as the disease process progresses. Gaining an understanding of pain, and the options for the management of pain, is extremely important. In this day and age, there is the medical capability to markedly diminish if not alleviate almost all pain. However, an unfortunate fact is that many people still spend their final weeks or days in unnecessary pain.

SCOTT AND DAVID

Scott, a writer and a poet, was given less than two years to live when he was initially diagnosed with bone cancer. Early in the course of his illness, following long discussions with his brother David and his wife, Julia, Scott had decided that he wanted to be as alert as he possibly could until he died.

He prided himself on his ability to observe life, and understand on a deep level what he was feeling, and what was happening with the people around him. His pain had not been so bad that it completely preoccupied him, and he had decided to take less, rather than more, pain medication early in his illness. He had meditated regularly for twenty years, and now said he wanted to put those skills to what he considered this "important test."

David was concerned that Scott would suffer needlessly—weren't there drugs that kept you pain-free, but still fairly alert? Also, David knew that Scott's early decision to be very cautious with pain medication was heavily influenced by having watched their father, Frank, die thirty years earlier.

Frank had died of liver cancer, and his last month alive had been agonizing for the entire family—he was alternately in pain, and on heavy dosages of morphine to control the pain. In the beginning they had to fight with the doctor to give Frank more pain medication, then later Frank seemed too drugged, and was in and out of a comalike state. Twice he had fallen into what looked like a coma, seemed to be near death, and they had called all the family to gather by the bedside. Then, like a miracle, he would wake up, and stay alive for weeks more.

David knew that Scott was afraid of following this same course, even though they both understood that approaches to pain management were much more sophisticated now. When they tried talking with Scott's doctor, however, he was dismissive. As a result, Scott shopped for a new oncologist, one who he was confident would work with him as a team, and take his concerns seriously.

Fortunately, he was able to find a doctor he trusted. They talked at length about the choices Scott would have in regards to pain control. Scott was relieved to learn that managing pain was more about juggling combinations of medications than simply going to higher and higher levels of morphine. He was also reassured to know that his doctor placed value on pain control techniques other than medication, such as meditation.

A few weeks before Scott died his pain began noticeably increasing. David again asked their doctor to talk with them both about what might be ahead for Scott. Their doctor understood that Scott was resistant to the idea of increasing the pain medicine, but she convinced him that they could control his pain, and keep him as alert as possible up until the end. She told Scott that pain was much more effectively controlled if kept at bay, rather than trying to reduce it, once it got bad. It might take a bit of medication juggling, and several dosage increases, but she assured them they would be able to get Scott comfortable most of the time.

The conversations David and Scott had with the doctor about pain control near the end of Scott's life were the hardest both had ever had. For both of them, it brought back the agony of watching their father in pain, and also brought up Scott's fear, until now unspoken, that he would be too drugged to say goodbye to David, and to other family members when he was near death. Scott was afraid the morphine would put him into a fog, and that he would die before he was ready to.

In those last two weeks of Scott's life, he slept more, but was alert, able to talk, laugh, and cry with David and Julia. He died with David holding his hand, only an hour after their last conversation.

Talk About Pain Management Early in the Illness

We all have concerns about how much pain there will be near death—ours and others. Many of us, like David and Scott, have watched other people in pain. The best remedy for your fears about pain is to get as much information as you can about what pain will likely be in the future for the dying person, and understand how it can be alleviated. If your doctor is not responsive to your concerns, find a new one; one who will collaborate with you.

ASK FOR DETAILS

We don't ask about pain often enough. This is because we tend to be afraid of even knowing the people we love are in pain. Also, sick people may be afraid of being seen as "complainers." So begin by asking about their level of pain, and when you ask, be as specific as you can. Question them in detail about any pain symptoms. This will reassure them that someone is paying attention to their care, and will also encourage them to be more alert to their own pain management.

With many illnesses, pain management becomes increasingly important as the illness progresses. Unfortunately, many physicians and nurses, while adept at the diagnosis and treatment of illness, are not well versed in the management of pain. There are several myths about pain management that continue to be perpetuated among medical professionals, despite current research and legislation.

Common myths are:

- Using narcotics early on in the treatment of pain will leave you with nothing to use later on when the pain is more severe.
- With long-term use of narcotics, there is a good reason to be concerned about addiction.

- Prescribing the high doses of narcotics that may be necessary to alleviate pain may hasten death and is equivalent to physician-assisted suicide.
- Prescribing high doses of narcotics over long periods of time is illegal.
- If patients don't look like they're in pain—fidgeting, grimacing, and so forth, or are able to concentrate on other things for periods of time, then the discomfort they are describing is probably psychological—depression, manipulation, or attention-seeking behavior.

All of these statements continue to be taught and believed by many well-meaning health-care providers. In this day and age, it is rare to be truly unable to control pain, or get someone's pain under control. Sometimes a person's pain can be managed with few or no side effects. Other times, with good pain control, there may be side effects, such as drowsiness or decreased level of consciousness. When the illness is far progressed and pain is more severe, the trade-off that you choose may be decreased alertness. Some people would rather tolerate mild to moderate levels of pain, in order to be fully awake and alert, and other people would far prefer to have all pain alleviated and sleep. The important thing is that the dying person is offered the choice.

How do you know if the dying person is receiving adequate pain management? A few guidelines:

- Check to make sure the health-care provider is asking often about pain.
- Ask (or check to make sure the doctor asks) detailed

and descriptive questions about pain. What is the location of the pain? What type of pain is it—sharp, dull, aching, or shooting? How about the intensity of the pain? How would you rate it on a scale of from zero to ten?

- Always believe what dying people say about their pain. Pain should be relieved. It may take combinations of medications, and constantly increasing doses to accomplish this.

- Never accept pain as a given—check to make sure the doctor continues any efforts to adjust medications, and how he administers them, until the person in pain says the pain is gone or at a level of comfort they are satisfied with.

- Use relaxation and distraction techniques in conjunction with medications.

Talking with Professionals

Don't assume that your doctor or other health-care providers will take the lead in talking about matters related to death. Physicians have long been trained in the science of healing, but this healing refers to the body, not the soul. Death, to many doctors, is the hallmark of failure, even though it is the guaranteed outcome of many illnesses. If you hear a doctor say, "There's nothing more we can do," this may be a red flag that he or she is not oriented toward total end-of-life care.

Of course, it *is* true that at some point in any illness there is no more medical treatment that will get that person to a healthier state. But you need to remember this: There is always more you can do to offer them comfort—and to ease their suffering.

Many health-care providers, doctors and nurses included, are uncomfortable talking about death. It quite simply isn't in their training! This means you may have to be the advocate for your loved one. Encourage her to allow you to attend doctor visits with her. We tend to be very focused on privacy in our society and we respect someone's right to privacy above all else. But, by attending visits with her, you can help her describe problems that have come up, and you can also remind her about questions you have both already discussed. By simply being present, you offer a second pair of ears to take in what the doctor says. Especially if the topic of discussion is emotionally difficult—as discussions about illness often are—it can be hard for the patient to remember what the doctor said after the fact.

If she wants time alone with her doctor, you can leave partway through the appointment. Before the appointment, write down any questions you have, so you remember to ask them. During the appointment, write down any specific instructions the doctor gives to her and you—this will help you both remember later, but will also force you to be very clear on any instructions for care and medications.

Questions you absolutely must have answered:

- What kind of symptoms, specific to this disease, should we expect?
- What potential problems should we watch for?
- If those problems come up, what can I (or others) do to ease the discomfort?

- What symptoms should I report to medical personnel promptly?

THE FINAL DAYS—VIOLET

Violet was seventy-six years old and had been fighting breast cancer on and off for seven years. She'd had a mastectomy, chemotherapy, and radiation therapy. Her doctor was originally optimistic about her prognosis, but four years later, the cancer reoccurred. This time the cancer had spread to several parts of her body, and she didn't respond as well to treatment.

Violet had varying amounts of support throughout her illness. Her husband, Ed, wanted her to do well, and drove her to appointments, but he couldn't tolerate talking about, or even thinking about, her cancer. Her oldest daughter, Valerie, also backed off from discussing death, and stressed the importance of remaining positive any time the topic came up. On the few occasions that Violet wanted to talk about her cancer, she turned to her younger daughter, Karen. They were close, and Karen was the one most willing to talk. It was Karen that Violet told she wanted to die at home, if at all possible.

Karen raised the topic of dying with Ed, knowing her mother would never be able to. Ed too wanted Violet to die at home, and he knew he could get some help from the hospice program, but he was still immobilized by the prospect of what lay ahead. He didn't want his wife to go to a nursing home. At the same time, he was fearful of her being at home—afraid she would need care he couldn't give; that crises would come up that he would manage poorly; and afraid that, ultimately, he would fail her.

After two family discussions facilitated by the hospital social worker, they all decided to give it a try caring for Violet at home with the help of hospice. If it didn't work out, then they would turn to the nursing home.

The first few weeks home went well. Ed would call Karen with questions and concerns on a regular basis, but usually could be easily reassured. After a few more weeks, Violet began going downhill noticeably. The pain in her back and right hip increased, and she began spending much more time in bed. Early on, Karen and Monica, the hospice nurse, noticed that when Violet's pain worsened, she became more anxious. This set off a cycle—Ed would get more anxious in response to Violet, which further increased her anxiety; as Violet got more anxious, she inevitably had more difficulty breathing. Sitting with her calmly, holding her hand, talking to her quietly, and encouraging her to breathe slowly usually helped settle her down fairly quickly.

Karen had always followed her mother's lead as Violet alternated between talking about her illness or talking about her plans for the future. Now, with the time of her death obviously near, and her mother saying little or nothing, Karen knew it was up to her to broach the topic of dying more directly than she had before.

"You never seem totally comfortable or relaxed, Mom. Are there things you're worried about?" Violet gave her typical response. "No, dear, I'm fine." But Karen knew her mother's stoicism, and was determined to go further this time. "You don't seem fine. What's on your mind, Mom?"

Violet was quiet for a while. "I'm afraid of dying," she finally said.

"What is it you're afraid of?"

At this point, Violet began to talk more than she had in a while. She talked slowly and quietly, pausing frequently to get her breath. She talked about her fear of the unknown, since she had never been a particularly religious person. She also talked about her concern for Ed. How would he manage alone? Karen was able to reassure her that Ed wouldn't be alone. Both she and Valerie would be there for him. Eventually, Violet was quiet, and Karen sat with her as she drifted off to sleep.

Over the next five days, which were the last of Violet's life, she drifted in and out of sleep. Following their talk, Violet had seemed less agitated, and also in less pain. She ate almost nothing, then stopped drinking as well. This was, again, a difficult step for those around her. They felt like they were letting her get dehydrated and starve to death, and doing nothing for her. Monica showed them how to keep Violet's mouth clean and moist, and encouraged them to support the natural process of dying.

Violet's skin got cool and blotchy-looking, just as was predicted in the pamphlet Monica had given them about what to expect near death. On the last day of her life, her breathing sounded very congested at first, then got very shallow, but she didn't seem uncomfortable. Her skin was very cool, and when she opened her eyes, she didn't seem to be looking at any of them. Monica said that the end was very near, and that although she was no longer talking, there was a good likelihood she could still hear.

They each took their time sitting with Violet and talking to her. Even Ed was able to tell her that he loved her and that he would be okay. Violet died very peacefully late that night, with both Ed and Karen at her side, and Valerie and her grandchildren sleeping in the rooms nearby.

The fear and loss of control that Ed felt can make the idea of talking with the dying person even more difficult than it already is. What specifically happens near death has a lot to do with the disease or illness the dying person has. However, many illnesses share common aspects of physical decline, especially in the final days and hours of life. Knowing more about some of the changes to expect can, and in Ed's case did, allay some of these fears.

Talking with somebody about their impending death is particularly difficult not only because the topic stirs up difficult emotions, but also because you may be entering into territory that you fear you know little about. If you haven't yet been closely involved with someone as they die, you may have questions and fears about what will happen to them near the end, and if you will be able to offer the help they need.

Near the time of death, or the time when people are described as actively dying, there are a number of changes you can expect to see in the person you are caring for. Her appetite will diminish altogether, as will her intake of fluids. Don't force fluids at this point, since the body no longer uses them near death, and they will only increase her discomfort or difficulty breathing by pooling in her lungs or other tissues. Also, she may lose the ability to swallow. To help her stay comfortable, give her ice chips, keep her lips moist, and give her good mouth care.

Her skin color and temperature will change. Her skin may look blotchy, and her fingers, toenails, and lips may take on a bluish hue. Her skin will probably feel very cool to the touch. As her body shuts down, her blood is still sent to her internal organs and brain, but less is sent to the periphery. You may see a much darker look to her skin on the side on which she is lying. This is, quite simply, the effect of gravity causing pooling of blood and fluid in her tissues.

Or she may be awake, but seem confused or delirious, and she may seem to see people who are not there. It is not uncommon for dying people to "see" and talk to people who have died before them. If she is agitated or confused, offer support by sitting quietly by her, touching her lightly. Place your hand on her arm, or take her hand, and maybe talk quietly to her. Don't bother putting much energy into trying to orient her, unless she seems particularly distressed. Any efforts you make to convince her of something different than she seems to be experiencing may only increase her confusion. She may grimace and moan. This is not necessarily related to any pain or discomfort. However, if she seems distressed by the disorientation, talk with her doctor about medication.

Breathing patterns also change near death. Oftentimes, breathing gets very labored and gurgly, sometimes referred to as "the death rattle." The fact that her breathing sounds congested does not mean that she is experiencing discomfort, especially if she is, overall, lying still. This is just the sound caused by the fluids in her body beginning to pool, as mentioned earlier. Her breathing may get very shallow, irregular, and stop altogether for stretches of many seconds. These irregular breathing patterns may go on for many hours before her breathing stops altogether.

During the final days or hours of her life, you'll see changes in her level of consciousness. She may be in a coma, or may be awake, but not seem responsive, and you may be unsure of whether or not she is aware of your presence and what you say. Remember that hearing is often the last of the senses to go—there is good evidence that people can hear long after they stop communicating. Whether or not she responds, take this final time to say the things that are the most important to you. Often, these include "I love you," "I'll miss you," and "It's all right to go, I'll be okay."

FOUR

The "Long Goodbye"

ॐ

Nothing is so strong as gentleness
and nothing is so gentle as real strength.
—RALPH W. SOCKMAN

In today's world, we live with many illnesses that have treatments but no cure. Illnesses such as AIDS, Alzheimer's, and
other dementias, some types of cancer, heart disease, and lung
disease may extend over long periods of time. In most of these
cases, people with these illnesses may go for many years when
death is not their, or your, as a caregiver, focus. You may both
know that the illness is incurable, but since modern medicine
can stave off the decline, most of the efforts, appropriately, go
into keeping life as close to normal as possible. Other than the
important discussions regarding advanced directives, the person with the illness, and any of their family and friends, may
seldom think about death and loss.

At some point, however, the dying person, and those who
are close to her, will begin experiencing more and more losses;
the first serious pneumonia with AIDS; a second heart attack;
or the first time your mother, who has Alzheimer's, forgets

your name. As these losses increase, everyone's attention to death—both physical death as well as all of the "little deaths" along the way, will increase. And for illnesses that do have a long course, these little deaths may be many, and over time, can take a heavy physical and emotional toll on both the sick person, and their caregiver.

When death, either psychological or physical, becomes a main focus of the ongoing and defining aspects of the experience of life-threatening illness, that experience has been described as the "long goodbye." If you are in the position of saying a "long goodbye" to someone you love, you know that coping with this situation poses particular challenges. Sometimes these challenges are due to the unpredictable course of the illness, as time and time again everyone braces themselves for death, only to have the sick person survive the crisis. Other types of challenges are due to the very real losses, or "minideaths," along the way.

Alzheimer's is the most common illness that routinely demands that goodbyes be said early, if they are going to happen. This is because the personality and abilities of the person with Alzheimer's change dramatically, *long before* their actual death. If you are caring for a person with Alzheimer's, you will need to say goodbye as early in the illness as possible. With many other long-term illnesses that do not involve dementia— heart disease, AIDS, or some cancers—the focus is often on hope, and on living, until close to the very end.

Alzheimer's disease poses many of the challenges of other long-term illnesses, plus some unique or exaggerated forms of loss. A lifetime of building a particular way of being with this person is altered. Caregivers are challenged daily to adjust to not only the enormous demands of the physical care, but also to the emotional demands of losing someone they knew well. At the same time, they need to be adapting to the new and ever-changing relationship.

Overall, the losses experienced by Alzheimer's patients, and their caregivers, are so many, and can be so profound, that their experiences in dealing with loss serve as excellent examples of how to deal with the losses in any long-term illness.

What Will Happen?

Uncertainty is difficult to tolerate. Waiting, watching, hoping, worrying. For many people, the uncertainty of life-threatening illness over a long period of time is one of the hardest aspects of the situation to tolerate. What do you brace yourself for? What do you hope for? How long can you manage? How can you "get on with life" when you are living in limbo, yet how can you not, since your life is, in so many ways, moving on?

SARAH
Sarah was managing to care for her husband, José, weathering one crisis after another. More than once, his doctor had told her that he probably wouldn't pull through, but he did. Each time, her sister would keep the all-night vigils with her at the hospital. Twice now, her children had dropped what they were doing—their jobs, families, and busy lives—to fly home and say their goodbyes. They had had a long and happy marriage, and Sarah desperately wanted her husband to live.

But more and more, she believed that he was never going to get much bet-

ter than this touch-and-go, crisis existence, and that this painful state was going to stretch on forever. More than once, she told her sister, "If I just knew what to expect, I could take it. But I never know what to expect one day to the next. I feel like I'm constantly walking through a minefield." She was hitting a point where she sometimes thought that she just wanted everything to end, that she was exhausted and couldn't take this any longer.

When she caught herself thinking this, she felt tremendously guilty— was she really wishing that this person she loved would die? What kind of woman was she? It was only in a state of total exhaustion that she, very tearfully, put these feelings, and her self-recriminations, into words.

The emotional roller coaster of the long goodbye is extremely draining. It demands holding contradictory information simultaneously. The sick person may seem pretty much the same one day as he was the day before. At the same time, you might be seeing little changes that you want to avoid noticing, or explain away as due to factors other than his illness. The changes, small and large, are nagging reminders of what you are losing. How do you balance the demands of illness and loss with the other aspects of your relationship with this person, and with any semblance of "normal" life?

Many illnesses have a somewhat unpredictable course, leaving us unsure time and time again of whether to brace ourselves for death, or invest in the hope for a more prolonged future with some quality of life.

Not only does modern medicine make it so that people are living longer with life-threatening illness, but people are living to much older ages, which has resulted in a significant rise in age-related illnesses, such as Alzheimer's disease. After the age of seventy, the risk of developing Alzheimer's disease increases dramatically with each passing year. This means that many, many people will be coping with a spouse, parent, or other aging family member with this progressive debilitating illness.

The emotional challenges of Alzheimer's are enormous—step by step the person you know and love changes, slipping further and further away. The relationship changes as the "mutual" aspect of your interactions diminishes. The ability to talk together, grieve together, and with this, support each other in shared experiences disappears long before the actual death.

This can be enormously painful and emotionally taxing. Preparing for, and sometimes even wishing for, a loved one's death at difficult times in the course of their illness can stir up feelings of guilt and betrayal. Yet trying to be optimistic about the future when the indication is that this may be futile can be very painful, and may feel next to impossible, or even wrong to do. Generally, these situations result in the caregivers having to tolerate, possibly for long periods of time, the experience of uncertainty.

The Demands of a Long-Term Illness

I first met Julie Noonan Lawson when I was putting together a workshop on Alzheimer's disease. Julie is a thirty-nine-year-old woman whose mother died of Alzheimer's disease twenty years ago. Her older sister, Fran, now has the disease, as does another sibling. Two more siblings are showing the early signs.

Julie asked that I use her real name when telling her story. Like so many people who find ways to cope with and make some kind of meaning out of tragedy and loss in their lives, she is finding her way. As she experiences so much loss in her family, she speaks out, in hopes that educating people about the disease and the effects on her family will help draw attention to Alzheimer's, and improve the supports available to people.

JULIE AND FRAN

Julie and her sister Fran were extremely close throughout her adult life, until several years ago when Fran started showing the personality changes brought on by her illness. She struggled to describe this change, the one that she and other family members saw long before the doctors could diagnose the illness.

"It's like an absence, and my sister Fran was always so verbal. As adults, she and I had developed a really close relationship, especially since we had our children at the same time. We could discuss anything. My relationship with her was the kind that you know you can completely rely on, that kind of core trust. And now she's gone, but she's not gone. In reality I can't talk to her, yet she's on the other end of the phone. It was like she decided she didn't want to be my friend anymore, as if she didn't like me, and I couldn't understand why. Even though I fully understand that the disease is the cause, emotionally it's different—it's like she's giving me the silent treatment. When people say to me, 'Remember that it's the disease,' it infuriates me. Because I do know it's the disease, and I find myself falling short continuously, thank you very much."

Julie talked about how the personality change that accompanies Alzheimer's disease—even more than the forgetting—can be one of the most difficult changes to accept on a daily basis.

"They may respond differently to situations. It's like having a friendship that you really valued and losing it. Fran and I could discuss anything. So *now, it's as if a piece of my heart has been carved out. We were so close, and if I had a fan in my life, she was it. She just loved me, and I felt that love. And now, she gets frustrated with me, and is less tolerant with me, and just doesn't have much appreciation for me. It's as though the relationship has reverted back to the time before we became close friends, like when I was young. It's such a huge loss."*

Understanding the loss doesn't take away the feelings. It is normal for our intellectual understanding of the person's changes and our emotional "understanding" to be very different. You need to have your feelings, and find your own way, in your own time, to work through them. Of course, you can understand what the doctor says, or what you can see about the illness, and how it has affected the person you love, and by extension you. But how significant these losses really are for you take time to bubble up from your psyche, and reveal themselves.

With Debilitating Illness, the Losses You Experience Are Very Pervasive

This is true for not only the loss of the person you care about, but also the loss of the relationship, and who you were in the relationship. Up until the illness, mutual needs and mutual gain defined your relationship. Long-term illness is guaranteed to alter the mutuality of your relationship, as the sick person's personality, ability to reason, and ability to care for herself will change entirely. Her ability to focus on and understand you may disappear completely. Who you are and can be in relation to her will change completely as well. So, with the multiple losses you experience, you end up losing not only the person you love, but aspects of yourself as well.

This process is usually slow and can be extremely painful. It involves role changes as well. Who does what in a relationship is based on the personalities and the competence of the people involved. For example, you grow up experiencing your parents in a certain way. You now may have reworked your relationship with them, since you are both adults and on the same playing field. Probably nothing has prepared you for needing to assume the decision-making role about their lives when their cognitive capacity becomes impaired, especially if their wishes for independence and autonomy are no longer in keeping with their ability.

Living under the threat of death, but knowing that, based on reasonable expectations, there is a lot of time left, often makes it difficult to know how to talk about the future. You may be sorely tempted to avoid the topic of death or the future altogether, believing that it can always be addressed "tomorrow." Too often, when tomorrow comes, you've lost the opportunity.

How We Cope with Progressive Illness

One of the ways that we tend to cope with difficult aspects of life is to find some way to maintain a sense of control. With a progressive illness, you might finally adjust to one set of problems or losses, only to have the next challenge pop up. You finally figure out how to manage a medication problem, or get help in place, when the visiting nurse switches agencies and is no longer covered by your mother's insurance. Or you find out your mother is having a mild adverse reaction to the new medication you at first thought was a godsend. Emotionally, you might be taxed in a way you never experienced before. You may see improvement, or at least stabilization, one day, and as soon as your hopes go up, have to face another major change, and dashed hopes, the next.

The physical demands of caretaking long-term are simply mind-boggling. Everything from the medical regime and appointments, to personal care, to daily living demands—getting the laundry and shopping done and paying the bills—still needs to be taken care of while your time is occupied with caretaking. Also, the sometimes enormous financial demands can be overwhelming when your expenses exceed your resources—adding an additional worry and threat.

"Make time for yourself" is frequent advice for caregivers. While it will certainly be helpful to you to carve out time for yourself, the advice can seem ridiculous. How can you possibly go to lunch with a friend, or to a movie, when you can barely make the time to take a shower? Yet, if you don't find a way to nurture or rejuvenate yourself, your ability to care for the sick person will diminish, no matter what your intentions.

What Should You Do?

Learn to pay attention to your feelings. The losses involved in long-term illness will stir up many, many feelings that are part of normal grieving. Feelings of sadness, anger, guilt, vulnerability, and helplessness are common. It is important to recognize these feelings as they arise. Pushing your feelings aside, censoring them, explaining them away, or believing that they are abnormal or a sign of weakness will simply use a lot of your energy, and will ultimately make them more difficult to cope with.

PAT

Pat, a sixty-year-old woman whose husband, Joe, had Alzheimer's, spent a couple of years feeling very guilty about the anger she felt at her husband as he followed her around, asking the same question over, and over, and over again. Understanding the limitations imposed by his illness, she would start out patiently, but inevitably would lash out at him when she could no longer stand it. The guilt she felt at her own inability to manage the situation the way that she thought she should only compounded the problem—she would feel angry at herself, then have less ability to respond to him in caring ways.

Pat struggled with this cycle for a few years until she came across a book on grief. "I read this book and I was amazed and relieved. It made sense to me that my anger was really a part of my grieving the loss of Joe."

What Pat was so angry about was not just the irritating repetitious questions, but more important, what these symbolized for her—the loss of her bright, intellectual partner. Once she understood that she was grieving, not just being some terrible person who was angry at someone who was ill, her anger actually diminished and the irritation she felt at his annoying new qualities was much more manageable.

Like Pat, Julie also had the experience of recognizing her feelings of grief as being liberating. When people point out to Julie that Fran's lack of tolerance, or inability to show appreciation for Julie, is simply due to the disease, Julie feels furious. "I want to strangle them," she said, "because, so what? I don't care. It still hurts. I'm still angry as hell. I'm still in pain as a result of the loss. So it's recognizing that loss, the continual loss, that helps. If I stay in touch with the ongoing loss, I do better than when I try to reason about the disease. It's been my saving grace in life to recognize that grief is all around me and very much a part of me, and the more I accept it as part of my life, the better I can function in my life. It started out in my own personal journey of just being aware of my feelings. Trying to be conscious of how I am feeling helps me to be more present and more alive."

Asking for Help

We live in a society that places great value on autonomy and independence. Being able to manage on our own is equated with strength and maturity. I constantly hear people struggle with what they think they should be able to handle on their own. However, no one can manage the demands of long-term illness—either the logistical or the emotional demands—alone. Not well, anyway. These same people inevitably believe that, due to some personal flaw, they are repeatedly coming up short. The problem is that their functioning is normal, but their self-expectations are unrealistic. We need supports and communities to manage the truly difficult aspects of caregiving.

If you find yourself having difficulty asking for help, or refusing offered help, ask yourself the following:

- What is getting in the way of my accepting help?
- Am I laboring under the misconception that I should be able to manage this by myself?

- Am I afraid that I will be a burden to others?
- What would it mean to my friends or family members to have the opportunity to help me right now?

Pat worked very hard at caring for her husband. She kept her children up to date on their father's status, and they visited as often as they could. Several times her adult daughter, Joan, offered to stay with her father so Pat could get away. Pat always declined, not wanting Joe's Alzheimer's to put more of a drain on their children than necessary. Finally, an important commitment came up, and Pat left town for a long weekend. Joan came and stayed with Joe.

When Pat returned, she realized that Joan really valued the opportunity to help care for her father, to whom she had always been very close. *Pat thought she was protecting Joan, but she was actually depriving her of an opportunity to give, one of the most important elements for establishing closeness in a relationship.* Look at some of the following suggestions for asking for help.

ASSIGN ONE PERSON TO ORGANIZE HELP FROM OTHERS

There are many details—simply to manage everyday life—that require our time and attention. When illness is added into the mix, it can be overwhelming. How do you care for a very sick person and get all the tasks done—the shopping, banking, laundry, cooking, chauffeuring, and on and on? Let's say you are fortunate enough to have a large support network. There is still one downside—organizing the help can be tricky.

There is a good book, *Share the Care*, listed in the Resources section, that details good ways to organize help when dealing with terminal illness so that the help you are receiving feels like just that.

IDENTIFY AVAILABLE SUPPORTS

Look beyond your personal support network to the larger community. There often are formal supports available if you know how to find them. There are many illness-specific organizations, such as the Alzheimer's Association or American Cancer Society, that have local chapters who will know of services and other resources in your area. Hospices often provide, or know of others who provide, respite services.

If you are involved in a community of worship, there are often people who are more than happy to give you a hand, or even to make the time-consuming phone calls to identify services. Looking into what is available in your larger community is especially important if you are trying to care for someone who lives at a distance.

TAKE THE TIME TO SET YOUR PRIORITIES

Really examine what is necessary and let things that are not truly necessary go. So often we go through our days and make our choices on automatic pilot. Many typical household tasks can go undone for long periods of time with no serious consequences, as long as there is food to eat and clothes that are clean enough to wear. Consider ways to streamline daily tasks, such as grocery shopping on the Internet, clothes shopping by catalogue, or, if finances permit, having laundry picked up and dropped off by a service.

Document a Life

Talk early in the illness about how to retain memories. Whatever the long-term illness, the healthy person you have known will likely change as a result of the illness.

If the person you are caring for is unwilling, or unable, to speak, find other ways to record, for your own memories, who they are. Stop for a minute and think about what it is about the person you love that you hold dear. It is most often whatever defines them as a unique person—their attitude, voice, touch, the way they look. Use your imagination to think of the ways you can capture who they are while they are still alive.

JAN AND CHARLES

Jan's father, Charles, has Alzheimer's disease that has progressed to the point where he has no language, no apparent recognition of his home surroundings, and no ability to engage in self-care. His decline has been slow, taking place over a number of years. Their family style has been to avoid all mention of the disease and go about life as if there were no changes. In retrospect, Jan wished that they had talked more when her father was first diagnosed, but she will be forever grateful for an idea that her mother carried out.

Her father was at a point where the changes from his illness were obvious. He was more forgetful, and much less focused than he ever had been before. He also seemed more vacant much of the time.

One night the family gathered in their much-loved vacation home. Jan's mother, Judy, took out the family scrapbook that contained pictures and mementos collected over the years. The pictures dated back to years before Jan and her siblings were born. As her father showed great delight in beginning to flip through the scrapbook, Judy turned on the tape recorder. She then taped the whole evening as he reminisced, and told all the family stories that the pictures or mementos reminded him of.

When Jan and I last spoke, her bright, articulate father no longer had any language. He uttered only repetitious, meaningless, single syllables. He no longer lived at home. Most of the time, he seemed to recognize her when she visited and when he did, he seemed happy to see her. But gone is the man who was her mentor, who believed in her and encouraged her. She still values her interactions with him. He is gentle, and takes pleasure in some of the activities they join together in. Yet she sometimes has trouble remembering him as he was, and finds that her memories are distorted by the man she interacts with now. When she puts on the tape, however, she is filled with joy and thinks, "Now, that's my father."

It's often very tempting with long-term illness to put off thinking about the inevitable. When someone is declining very slowly, you may avoid the idea of death, thinking you can wait until tomorrow to address any issues around the end of life. While the idea that you have time may be true in some ways, in other ways it couldn't be more wrong.

Changes in a person may occur very slowly over time and, day to day, the changes may be difficult to notice. However, the person you love *is* changing, and the opportunity to document him or her in the ways that you want to remember them will be gone forever. You will notice that what you remember of the sick person, changes as the sick person progresses in their illness. It can be a struggle to keep the memory of who your loved one was alive over time. If your mother has Alzheimer's, for example, your day-to-day experience of her will play a role not only in how you think of her now, but in who you remember her to be after she dies.

Take any opportunity you have before the person's illness is far progressed to document who she is. Audiotapes and videotapes are wonderful ways to record your memories. Writing down family stories, especially ones that capture something characteristic about the person, is another way.

Thoughts and Decisions About Suicide

When people are facing a long and debilitating illness, it is common for them to have intense feelings about the road ahead. These feelings can include fears about many things— loss of control, dependence, loss of who they see themselves to be, how others will see and subsequently remember them, and, often, that they will be a burden on those who love them and will be caring for them.

Imagine yourself in their situation. What would cross your mind? Many people with life-threatening illnesses think, at some point, about ending their life earlier than the illness will. Especially if they have an illness that involves a slow and debilitating progression.

JULIE AND FRAN

Among the things that Julie Lawson looks back on and is glad for are the conversations she had with Fran about the option of suicide. Since their mother had died of the same illness, both Fran and Julie knew, all too well, what lay ahead once Fran developed Alzheimer's. When it became clear that Fran had the disease, she, initially, didn't want to live. No one was willing to talk with her about this except Julie.

They talked a lot over the year following the diagnosis about Fran killing herself, often using humor as a way to manage the magnitude of the painful feelings they were grappling with. Instinctively, Julie knew that Fran needed to be able to express these feelings. Eventually, through their talks, Fran came to realize that suicide was not an option she would choose. Aside from her own needs, she has two adolescent children. Suicide, as a way to handle pain and difficulty in life, was not the example she wanted to set for them.

Thanks to her talks with Julie, Fran decided against the option of suicide, she also became clearer on how she did want to handle things. Knowing what may come, Fran decided to let nature take its course. She made it clear to all who love her the point at which she wants all medical efforts to go into maintaining her comfort, with no life prolonging treatment. When the time comes that she is no longer able to feed herself, she wants no spoon-feeding, or any other way of getting nutrition or fluid into her. This is a choice that everyone understands and is prepared to help her with.

In addition to helping Fran, their talks also helped Julie. The fact that she is able to support Fran in a way that Fran very much needs gives her some consolation. It also affects the way that Julie thinks about her own possibilities. Since her family has the hereditary form of Alzheimer's disease, she knows that she too may develop this illness within the next decade. All of her conversations with Fran helped her think about her own life, and what she wants to teach her children.

Listening to someone you love talk about suicide can be very painful, but it can also be very helpful. If he or she is talking about possibly committing suicide, don't hesitate to get outside help—call their doctor or other involved professionals. Thinking about suicide as an option for the future, however, is a different matter. The idea of becoming very sick and dependent, or being in pain, brings up fears for many people of being out of control and helpless. The idea of suicide offers a sense of control, the option of a quicker way out if life becomes, for any reason, intolerable.

Talk with the sick person about their thoughts concerning suicide should they bring it up—it will offer them a valuable opportunity to sort through their feelings about their wishes and fears for the end of their life. When someone is terminally ill, it's common for them to *think* about their ability to hasten their dying. It is rare, however, for terminally ill people to actually choose suicide.

Talking about suicide, and sharing the fears that stimulate these thoughts, helps people join together more closely and support each other, which diminishes one of the primary fears of the dying—that of being alone. These discussions can give the dying person an opportunity to examine what they do and do not want for the end of their life. They can also be an opportunity for you both to think together about all the ways these wishes and fears may be addressed, or alleviated, *other* than through suicide. There are many ways to end suffering other than ending the life of the sufferer.

Caring and Coping from a Distance

One of the very difficult things in today's society is that families often live spread over a wide geographical area. This makes things difficult in many ways, but probably no way more so than when a person you love is sick. Distance makes dealing with all illness difficult, but it is especially hard with long-term illness. If someone you love is critically ill, although it will pose many difficulties, you can drop what you're doing, get on the plane or a bus to see him, and to help, if necessary.

When the illness is long-term, however, this is much more challenging. What do you do with an ailing parent who is, over a long period of time, requiring more and more physical care when you live hundreds of miles away? And how do you get the full story, without actually being there? Especially if he is used to being independent, you may constantly be told by him on the phone that he is fine. You may be hearing from other people, however, that this is not the case. You may get phone calls from health-care providers, neighbors, or siblings with contrary information. Or, depending on your parent's personality, he may tell you that he desperately needs you, when you know that this hasn't usually been the case.

There are no easy answers for the problems of living far away during a long-term illness. Life is busy and has many demands, obligations, and commitments. Children are in school, people at work depend on you, and there are the financial realities of not being able to take time off and jump on a plane whenever you like. It may seem that the latter is the only "correct" choice to make, and at the same time it seems clear that it is one of the only options that is not possible.

As with everything else, every choice will mean gains and losses. Once again, the important thing is that you weigh out everything involved, and make your choices carefully and consciously. Get very concrete, and make lists of pros and cons for the different options—you'd be amazed at how very helpful simply writing your options down can be. Above all else, don't let feelings of guilt result in your pulling away or hesitating to offer what you can, believing that what you can realistically offer is too limited to really make a difference.

Your siblings, for example, may be picking up most of the parental care if they live nearby, and may be resenting the lack of your presence. A phone call may fall short of what you would like to be able to offer, but it still can be helpful—it keeps you involved, and you can offer a listening ear. Or money, for example, can help provide additional home care or respite care to ease the burden on those who are closer by.

Think carefully about what you need in regards to time spent together—if you don't go visit soon and his health declines significantly, will you regret your choice? It is the rare meeting that is cancelled or work deadline not made that we look back on for years with regret. Missed opportunities in relationships, however, stay with us for a long time.

The Opportunity Within the Losses

What so many people have shared with me is this—that the horrible situation they found themselves in made them stop and think about what they wanted to do, or say, while they had the chance. And for having, and using, that last chance, they were grateful

PHILLIP AND MARIAN

When Phillip's doctor determined he had Alzheimer's disease, the diagnosis hit him and his wife, Marian, hard. Although they had been seeing changes for years—he was forgetful, more irritable, distracted, disorganized—they

thought he was depressed due to midlife changes and some serious work problems.

Marian was devastated and wanted so much to talk with Phillip. She knew that the time they had left where they even could talk together was limited. But Phillip, who had never been much of a talker, especially around emotional topics, couldn't tolerate it. As Marian thought about all she was losing, she desperately wanted to share with Phillip all he meant to her. Over the years, she had been quick to focus on things that fell short in their relationship, and all the things that made her angry. Now many of these things seemed inconsequential. She was so much more aware of all the positive ways that their relationship had defined her world.

Phillip continued to noticeably decline. One day on the way out of church, which Phillip still attended regularly, their minister invited them to come talk with her. She could tell that Marian and Phillip needed help. By this time, Phillip had few really coherent conversations, though he often seemed to understand what went on around him. The day they met with their minister was one where Phillip seemed particularly clear.

As they sat in her office, Marian started to describe what was going on with Phillip's illness. She talked about all of the losses, choosing her words carefully so as to not upset him. Soon, however, she shifted her focus, and began talking with the minister, who had been with their church only a few years, about the man Phillip had been over the years.

She talked about all of the qualities that had made him a great father and husband. She talked about how hard he had worked to provide a certain lifestyle for their family, and she talked about who their children had grown up to be under his influence. Although Phillip had never been able to tolerate Marian saying these kinds of things to him in the intimacy of their private conversations, he sat there quite comfortably listening to her as she addressed a third party.

Marian left the meeting feeling both relieved and grateful. She finally felt like she had been able to say what she wanted to, to Phillip, in a way that he liked hearing it. Even now, after Phillip's death, when she looks back on that conversation, she feels good.

Most of us think of "opportunity" as something that we seek out and welcome, and any of us would trade in every secondary gain, without a moment's hesitation, if we could have back the health and life of the people we love. But we can't do that.

Many times, I've heard people reflecting back on the time they had with the person they love before they died, when they knew death was real, as a very special time. "In some ways, it was the best time in our relationship," or "We got closer during that time than we ever had been before." They gained precious moments, created togetherness, or got to know sides of themselves and the person they love that they had not previously seen. There may be things that surprise you, or touch you, if you make time with the person you love a priority, and put your effort into connecting, rather than pulling away.

JAN AND CHARLES

Jan had always heard what a good dancer her father had been when he was younger. It was a side of him that she had never seen, however.

By the time Jan got married, her father had had Alzheimer's for over five years, and much of his former personality was gone. This university professor could no longer carry on a conversation, although he was still mild-natured and easy to please. At the beginning of the wedding reception, he seemed confused by all of the commotion and the strange environment. He sat at the table where he had been placed. When the band started up, however, his face lit up, he stood up, grabbed her, and pulled her onto the dance floor. He danced with her, her mother, her new mother-in-law, and just about every other woman present. Jan's worry about how he would be able to manage the event melted away as she took delight in seeing this side of her father. Here was a moment, amid all of the loss, where a former side of him came forward, and is now part of the father she knows and will always remember.

The Little Things Define and Enrich Our Relationships—Small Gestures Leave a Profound and Lasting Effect

Why is it that this time of such adversity is also a time that can hold so much promise? For many, it is because they are aware in a new way that there won't always be more tomorrows. The diagnosis of life-threatening illness makes you stop and take stock of what is important, and what you have and haven't done or expressed. For all of the downsides to long-term illnesses, they do give you the time to express yourself in ways you have not yet done. Unlike a short illness, where everyone is in crisis mode, you have time to make your choices.

JULIE AND FRAN

Fran had always been very close to Julie's children, as she had to Julie. She knew she held a very special place with them and she did not want them to lose that because of her illness, so she had a lot of conversations with them about dying. One summer, when up at their family's summer lake home, Fran, Julie, and her two daughters went out for a canoe ride. They stopped along the shore, climbed out on some rocks, and sat looking at the mountains and all the beauty around them. Fran looked up into the clouds and started talking to the girls, telling them, "When you wish that you could talk to me, when you feel out of touch with me, I want you to look up to the clouds and talk to me, and I'll be listening to you."

Julie feels like she will be forever thankful to Fran for that moment. It is something that Fran, who can no longer have an intelligible conversation, cannot do today, but it is something that her daughters will have always.

FIVE

Even Difficult Relationships Require Goodbyes

The bitterest tears shed over graves are for words
left unsaid and deeds left undone.
—HARRIET BEECHER STOWE

Difficult relationships, in particular, can challenge you to really think about how you feel, and what you want to say, if anything, to a person when he or she is approaching death. There is no formula for talking. What you say is an outgrowth of how you think and feel, and in difficult relationships sometimes you may feel very torn and lost when you are challenged to interact with someone who is dying.

What does "difficult" mean? It means you've had a hard enough time communicating with, or reaching an understanding with, the other person that the relationship felt painful much of the time. It may mean that you frequently felt unvalued, unseen, disrespected, or out and out harmed. Or it may mean that you believe you have not treated the person well, and have feelings of shame or guilt.

Whether that relationship for you involved abuse of some sort, neglect, indifference, or perhaps long-standing animosity doesn't matter. "Difficult" means you feel confused about what to say to someone important to you near the end of his or her life.

How can you make the right decision—to not speak or to speak? And what do you say? Is there a right decision? These kinds of questions are probably similar to the kinds of indecision and soul-searching you've already had about the relationship throughout its turbulent history, and now that the end is imminent, your feelings come to the fore. How can you make decisions you feel comfortable with; decisions you will live with for the rest of *your* life, in the midst of this chaos?

You can begin by taking the pressure off yourself to "do the right thing." It is natural that tough relationships can set you spinning when it looks like you may only have one more shot at whatever it is you want to do—set things right, get an apology, apologize, reconnect with someone you have separated from, or express something important that has long gone unsaid. All goodbyes require your focus and a careful review of your feelings and motivations; especially goodbyes in difficult relationships.

The More Difficult the Relationship, the More Difficult the Grieving

Most relationships pose some difficulties, but some are truly abusive. We often think, especially if the person was abusive in any way, that their death will be less painful than if the relationship had been loving and close.

You may have wished for the person to be *out* of your life many times; you may have even wished him or her dead. You may have cut off contact years ago, or had only limited contact. Sometimes you may think that when they die the whole emotional struggle will finally be out of your life forever. This hope may help you cope in the moment, but actually couldn't be more wrong.

We often talk about "cutting ties" with people who have hurt us. Rarely do we cut ties. We cut off *contact*, but the ties remain strong. Ties are emotional, and, in one form or another, last a lifetime, and beyond. In fact, it is because the ties remain strong that contact has to be cut, or limited, in order to lessen the destructiveness of the relationship. What was meaningful once stays meaningful, even when its place in our life changes.

While it is not necessarily more painful, it *is* more complicated to approach the death of someone you've had a troubled relationship with, and it is more complicated to sort through what to say to that person at the end of their life.

If you have had a troubled relationship with someone, you likely carry a mix of those feelings—sadness, anger, avoidance, or a longing to make things different—into your interactions with them. Start by recognizing what they are. We are all emotionally complex, and the feelings we have associated with troubled relationships can be especially tangled and tough to sort out. The path toward sorting them out will be easier if you begin by identifying your feelings.

Established patterns of interaction are not easy to change. It takes work, and can feel uncomfortable. In difficult relationships, especially ones with family members or long-time friends, you likely have well-established patterns for how you relate to one another, and you may feel you have more to lose (than if the person were an acquaintance) if you try and break out of those patterns.

Patterns of relating and talking can help you feel safe; they can protect you from getting into verbally uncertain territory that brings up past hurts or unspoken desires. But they can also be unproductive, and stifle your ability to say what you would like to. Expect some discomfort as you try and break out of your established patterns.

After reflection, it helps to practice what you want to say. Practice talking about your feelings with others who can give you feedback; people that you trust. In our society, we are so used to avoiding discussions of death that we simply do not have many models for how to talk with each other about death—either for purposes of telling another we care for them, and will miss them, or for dealing with the practical issues of pain relief, or last wishes. In difficult relationships, communication is always problematic—a lack of understanding between you and the other person is part of what makes the relationship hard or painful. So conversations with this person will be more challenging.

It may be helpful for you to start those discussions with friends, relatives, or professionals, such as a social worker or psychologist. In this way, you will gain a greater understanding of your feelings, and what you would like to accomplish in speaking with someone near death—especially in situations that make you uncomfortable. Sometimes what is most important for us to say is also most difficult, and we need practice.

As you read the stories in this chapter, you will see ways in which people go about making careful choices that work for them. Even in the midst of hurt, anger, guilt, confusion, and chaos, you can stop and think about how you feel and what you want, and prepare yourself emotionally for how to act or what to say, if, indeed, you say anything at all.

CARRIE

Carrie had had no contact with her father since her mother died six years earlier. Cutting off contact had been a very difficult decision for her to make. Growing up, she was always her father's "little princess." But this special role had a very dark side. All their father-daughter "dates" to movies and museums and the times she went with him on business trips to exotic places had also been when her father sexually abused her.

Carrie managed to graduate high school in three years to get away from the house. When she was twenty-seven, she finally went to see a therapist, and over the next five years, she struggled to get out from under her negative self-image that had been so profoundly influenced by the abuse.

When Carrie was thirty-three, her mother died suddenly from a heart attack. While at home after her mother's funeral, the familiar battle with her father began. He told her he loved her and needed her. In years past this pattern of relating to her had led to sexual abuse. Carrie tried telling him how much he'd hurt her, but, as before, he was dismissive. And, as before, her anger erupted and she left. Finally, Carrie decided the only way she could avoid getting pulled in again, especially knowing he was alone, was to sever contact with him.

Six years after she had cut off contact, her father called to say he had pancreatic cancer, was doing poorly, and wanted to see her.

Carrie felt totally unprepared to cope with this new challenge. What about her resolve to have no further contact? She wasn't sure, but was afraid she might regret it if she didn't go see him. She knew she needed to figure this out. To help her sort out her feelings, Carrie returned to the therapist she had seen years ago.

"My therapist suggested I ask myself, 'Why am I still so attached to him?' I've always felt slightly ashamed that I struggled at all with not having contact with someone who hurt me so terribly. She asked me to write out a list of both good and bad things about my father.

"I looked at the list and realized that some of the good things about him—like how much he loved art and museums—made me think about the ways I'm like him. At first I was a little freaked out."

Weighing the pros and cons, Carrie decided to make the three-hour trip to see her father. She wasn't sure what she was going to say when she saw him.

"When I got to the hospital, he was sleeping and I was glad I didn't have to talk to him right away; I was shocked at how horrible he looked. He was surprised to see me when he woke up—I didn't say anything at first and neither did he. Finally he gave me his hand and said, kind of quietly, 'Thanks for coming.' I told him I needed to. That afternoon and then the next morning he slept a lot, and when he was awake, he asked about me—what I did for work, my friends, and what I'd been doing since Mom died. I wasn't really expecting more than small talk, but then he said, 'I'm sorry for all that I did when you were young.'

"I was surprised. All those years I wanted an apology, and now that I had it, it didn't feel like I expected it to. If it had come earlier, maybe it would have felt different, but then I just thought, 'Is this another selfish gesture on your part—trying to get rid of your guilty conscious at the last minute?'"

She was angry, but she "realized I really didn't care what his motivation was for apologizing—it was more honest than he'd ever been before. I told him, 'Thanks, it's good to finally hear you say you're sorry.' I also told

*him how I'd figured out I was like him—that I thought I was a good jour-
nalist because the world he showed me sparked my curiosity. He didn't say
anything for a long time when I told him that, but he looked very sad, and
he took my hand."*

His dying allowed both Carrie and her father to approach
their relationship differently. Carrie acknowledged that it felt
awkward to be that honest with her father, but remembered
thinking, "What do I have to lose?" She also said she left the
hospital feeling freer than she had in a very long time. The relationship had shrunken down to size somewhat. Her father
no longer seemed like the idol he had been when she was little, nor was he the powerful villain he had become in her late
adolescent and adult years. She felt clearer about why, despite
his cruelty, and the anger she felt toward him, she still loved
him. For this, she felt a little more normal.

PAY ATTENTION TO THE GOOD
ALONG WITH THE BAD

Rarely are we in relationships that are all bad. Take time to
think about what it is about this person, if anything, you find
admirable, or attractive. It will be time well spent, especially if
most of your time spent thinking about the relationship has
focused on how you were hurt, what you didn't get, or how
you have been damaged. You may well have been terribly and
unfairly hurt in the relationship, as was Carrie. But if it were as
simple or one-sided as this, you wouldn't be struggling now.
You clearly have reasons for considering trying to connect
with this person one last time. As Carrie did, ask yourself what

those reasons are, and why this person is important to you. Knowing what is important to you about this person will help you make decisions about what to, or what not to, say.

BE TRUTHFUL IN WHAT YOU SAY,
BUT KEEP IT SIMPLE

No matter what you do or say, you are not necessarily going to get the person to understand things about you, or about their behavior, they have not been able or willing to before. Also, a defensive or angry posture rarely leads to productive or satisfying interaction. It is more likely to keep old, problematic patterns going, and saying goodbye will feel as difficult and painful as the rest of the relationship has. You will often do best if you make simple, truthful statements about your own experience; statements that don't invite a lot of the old dialogue or focus on the old anger.

Use simple statements that acknowledge past harm—"I was very hurt by what you did to me," or "I felt alone and afraid when you were drinking." These statements set the stage for then expressing the positive aspects of the relationship, without feeling like you are denying the negative aspects. This is exactly what Carrie did when she told her father he had left her with good traits, while also being honest about the pain he caused her.

DO YOUR HOMEWORK/REVIEW YOUR OPTIONS

It wasn't neat and easy, but over the years Carrie had gotten therapy to work through the effects of the abuse. When it came time to make a decision to reestablish contact with her father at the end of his life, she had some emotional tools to work with; some understanding of how to take care of herself in that situation. Then, before she visited her father, she prepared herself by reviewing her options, both verbally with friends, and with her therapist, and on paper (with her lists).

Finally, she made a decision to be direct with her father, no matter how uncomfortable, and no matter the outcome. Because of her preparation, when Carrie was in the midst of the situation in her father's hospital room, she was better able to handle the flood of feelings that followed his apology, say what she needed to, and accept the outcome, whatever it was.

If You Have Been Sexually or Physically Abused

Our emotional attachments are very complex. Many times, our important relationships are difficult ones. Parents bring children into the world and are supposed to raise and nurture them, but they don't always have the tools to do a very good job. Since as children we're dependent on our parents, we stay emotionally connected to them, even when they hurt us. And since very young children see themselves as responsible for what goes on in their world, when a parent is neglectful or abusive, the child doesn't see it as being about the parent's shortcomings, but rather, as about their own worth. Children do not see parents as unloving; they see themselves as unlovable. These beliefs become an integral part of their identity.

As children mature, their intellectual ability to understand their relationships expands, but the deep-seated beliefs they incorporated about themselves early in life remain. The process of reworking these beliefs is difficult—and in varying ways will go on over a lifetime. For children who got the message that they were unlovable, or unworthy of being protected, this reworking is especially complicated and, usually, painful.

Their wish to *finally* get the relationship to be a loving one is very strong. But since the problem lies with the parent, it doesn't matter how hard the child (or adult) tries to change the situation. You can worry and puzzle over situations that have disturbed you, and you can change yourself and the way you interact with the abusive person, hoping for a different, more loving response. You can, and probably often do, agonize over what to "say," thinking if you can just get it right, they will understand your pain and be there for you in some way.

This rarely works because it isn't that you need to be different to be more lovable, understood, or cared for, it's that your parent has problems he or she needs to address. Any efforts you made (as a child or as an adult) to get that parent to change were probably fruitless—*you can't change another person, especially one who isn't looking to change.* Your abusive or neglectful parent was in a very powerful position, and as a child, probably even still as an adult, you may feel a strong pull to strive for their approval or love, in words and actions, in order to gain a sense of self-worth.

You are likely to feel this same dynamic and accompanying sense of hopelessness when you are worrying over *what to say* in especially difficult relationships. *Especially if the emotional pull to the abusive person is still very strong.* Even very destructive relationships have positive aspects that play a role in the emotional attachment. If your parent or parents were abusive, it is likely they also had qualities you liked and emulated, and that have become a positive part of your personality—Carrie loves how competent she feels as a journalist, a career choice heavily influenced by her father.

Your efforts to let go of the destructive aspects of a relationship often trigger the feeling that you will not only lose all connection to the person, but that you will also lose parts of yourself—parts that *you like about yourself*. This may seem like a hellish maze that, despite your best efforts, you cannot find your way out of. But it doesn't need to. When you pay attention to the dynamic between you and your parent, and get the kind of support you need from others (either through therapy, friends, or other family members), it is possible to sort through the relationship. You can hold on to the parts of yourself you like, but still distance yourself—in words and actions—from the old pulls that feel very negative or destructive.

Do your emotional homework before you talk with the person. Difficult relationships require your focus and a careful review of your feelings and motivations. If you do this work, you will be entering the situation as well equipped as possible to have an outcome you feel positive about.

There is never an exact formula for what to do, or say, and no tidy way to set really difficult relationships right—you can plan all you want, but in the end (no pun intended), you will do the best you can.

Code of Silence

In many families where there is abuse or neglect, children learn very early on the unspoken family rule that what is really going on in the family is *never to be spoken about*. Abusive or neglectful parents, however violent, rageful, controlling, or powerful, are also, in a certain kind of way, very fragile—they cannot tolerate much that stresses or challenges them. Children realize their parents will not be able to protect them, or provide safe environments, and that they can easily fall apart or be provoked to anger and violence.

In this volatile situation, children work hard to protect their parents—to help them feel okay. They pretend everything is all right, or that they are okay, when, in fact, they are not. Many children watch while one parent stays silent, and the other parent is verbally and/or physically abusive to any and all family members. This reinforces the child's learning that keeping quiet about what is *really* happening to them and other family members is important, not only to maintain safety, but often, as a matter of survival.

PATRICK

Patrick grew up in an abusive family. His mother drank heavily and his father withdrew, suffering in silence, until his retirement, when he too began drinking very heavily. At age sixty-seven, years of heavy smoking caught up with his father and he was diagnosed with emphysema.

"My dad knew he was on the way out. He was on oxygen and he'd had his cigarettes taken away from him, so he drank. I'd help him with his physical care—shaving him, cutting his nails, and cleaning him up some. I'd always find new bruises or cuts and scrapes and I'd bandage them. He fell down a lot because he was weak or drunk or both. That was how we spent his last year."

In Patrick's family, silence was the rule—that's how it had always been in the family, and that's how it was when his father was dying.

"We were more action- than talk-oriented, especially around family stuff and his dying. Our whole foundation is based on not saying anything to anybody. Silence. Don't hurt yourself, and don't hurt a family member. Everyone protecting everyone else. Things were really bad when I was a kid. We all knew it, but it was like we all also knew we had to pretend things were fine. One of my clearest memories from when I was little was my dad asking me, 'Are you okay?' and I said, 'Yeah,' and he knew that I was lying, and everyone knew, but that was the answer he wanted.

"While I was caring for my father, because of that silence, I never left there feeling really swell. He was always glad to see me, and could say that, but beyond that didn't say too much. It was a huge acknowledgment for him to say to me at one point—we were out sitting on the back porch—'You know, we haven't had the happiest of families.' I was thrilled to hear it, but it was maddening because it was such an understatement.

"Another time I was shaving him and he looked me right in the eye because we were in close contact, and he said, 'You know, I'm really proud of what you've done with your life.' It seemed like he was eager to say it, but he had to dig for it. And he had been waiting—he picked his moment. I said, 'Thanks, Dad, that means a lot.'"

With the help of his friends, Patrick had worked hard to break the patterns of silence learned in his family. Yet, when he was with them, he was back into it. He felt some regrets for not having broken through that fear and anger more often during his father's last days.

"If I could turn the clock back, there are things I'd do differently. I especially wish I had said more. My father did some great stuff. In a really messed-up family, I got out in one piece. He taught me a lot of wonderful things. And I never directly said thank you. I only did it in actions. I would like to have told him how much I appreciated him."

As Patrick discovered in his family, the unspoken rule in families with a code of silence at work is that the truth must never be spoken, for it will challenge, or break apart the fragile structure of the family. In this way, children grow up learning, without ever being told, that speaking their own truth may be very dangerous. This deep-seated belief will carry forward with the child into adult life.

This dynamic adds an additional challenge to saying goodbye. How can you say goodbye when it feels like acknowledging the reality of the history of the relationship would be dangerous? Pay close attention to this aspect of your experience when you are making choices about what to say and not say as you say goodbye, and remember the following:

- Even when, as an adult, you have worked hard at moving beyond this emotional stance in your adult relationships with friends or intimate partners, this relational pattern will often still be there when you are interacting with family members. *You* may have grown beyond the rules of how you related in your family, but other family members, including the dying person, often have not. Or you may slip into your role pattern out of habit.
- Express what you need to, but avoid setting yourself up for failure or renewed pain by assuming that your family member will tolerate you changing the rules.
- What you choose to say to the dying person may be very brief or clipped, as it was between Patrick and his father, but it can still give you a way of connecting. With this, you may be able to attain a level of acceptance or acknowledgment that is based on the experience of clearly sharing an aspect of your own truth.

DOING WHAT FEELS RIGHT—JESSIE

Jessie had been married for thirty-two years to her husband, Frank. Frank was a large, loud, intimidating man, who drank heavily and had always been self-centered. They had very little experience in sharing good times, and they rarely talked with each other, except to manage daily tasks, such as meals.

When Frank developed lung disease, he refused to give up smoking and drinking. And he was insistent on Jessie caring for him. Within weeks of each hospital discharge, he refused the continuation of nursing services. Finally, during his last hospitalization, the doctors said there was little they could do for him, and he no longer belonged in the hospital. If they kept him longer, his insurance company would refuse to pay.

His options were either to go home or to a nursing home. The doctor also talked with them about hospice. Frank was adamant that he wasn't going to any nursing home. Jessie, he said, would take care of him like she always had. Jessie wasn't so sure. She was fed up, and had a sense of what lay ahead—endless battles.

With some urging from friends, Jessie agreed to ask for help from the local hospice, despite Frank's protests. The hospice sent in a home health aide three mornings a week to help get Frank cleaned up for the day. The time Jessie most looked forward to in her week was the visit from the hospice social worker, Marilyn. At first she tried to paint a rosier picture of hers and Frank's relationship than she believed to be true. But as she got to know Marilyn better, she became more honest. Jessie admitted to Marilyn that she hated him at times, and more than once, wished he would die.

"One afternoon Marilyn asked me, 'Why are you doing this?' I told her I didn't feel like I had a choice. It just didn't seem right to abandon someone when they're dying. Marilyn pointed out to me that I was making a choice.

I was taking care of Frank because of a sense of obligation, but also because of what I believed was right."

Frank's final few weeks were hard—his breathing became slowly more difficult, and his congestion and coughing increased. During one of his more comfortable periods, Jessie tried to talk with him about their marriage and the time they had spent together. Even though he was weak and close to death, he was every bit as unreceptive to her efforts as he had ever been.

"I started out talking about how long we'd been together, and all he said was 'No kidding.' I kind of ignored that, and told him that I thought we'd had some good times, and I thanked him for always providing for our son and me. What I said made him uncomfortable, and he said, 'Jesus Christ, Jessie. Who cares about that now!'

"At first I felt angry and hurt, but it was just Frank, and not a surprise. When I think about it now, I'm proud of myself for taking good care of him despite his abuse. I know I did the best I could."

Jessie did do the best she could in an extremely difficult situation, and she was relatively pleased with the outcome. You may not always be happy with the outcome of a situation, but if you are pleased with the effort and attention you have put into it, you will most likely not be left with many unresolved feelings about "What could I have done?"

Don't try to do a lot of repair work by hashing through all the old anger at their bedside. Anger is a strong reaction to that which has hurt us. It also keeps us tightly connected to the person we are angry at, and perpetuates difficult and repetitive patterns of interaction. Ongoing anger will keep you hooked into the old destructive patterns where the person has power over you and, as such, has the power to hurt you.

Jessie had many angry feelings toward Frank, yet she realistically chose to turn her attention to the legacy she wanted to leave for herself in the relationship—that she had behaved generously despite hostility and indifference, and at the same time never denied her complicated feelings.

Not All Difficult Relationships Are Overtly Abusive

It is not only overtly abusive relationships that can be difficult. Even relationships with friends or mentors may be complicated. If you are struggling with a conflictual relationship, you are likely to find that many of the issues described in this chapter apply to you or describe your emotional experience, even though the hurt you experienced may have been from interactions that are more subtle than overt abuse.

For example, you may have been in a relationship that was characterized by a history of neglect, or of dynamics that always left you feeling criticized, devalued, or unloved. A relationship you have either distanced yourself from, or cut off altogether. These relationships—with friends, mentors, parents, or partners—can stir up many of the same emotional struggles or self-esteem issues that exist in more obviously abusive relationships.

Any relationship you step into with both feet—oftentimes, the people you call "family"—where the pulls are the strongest is likely to tap into deeply seated self-views.

NED
Ned's father had all but abandoned him when he was seven years old and his parents divorced. His father moved to a neighboring state. Within a year

or two, he remarried and went on to have two more children. His contact with Ned was sporadic and consisted of many unfulfilled promises. Many times, his father talked about wanting to spend time with him, but rarely followed up on his promises.

As an adult, hurt by the rejection and lack of forthcoming love, Ned had little contact with his father and made little effort to have his children get to know him. Ned made what he believed to be the obligatory phone calls on his father's birthday and holidays, but all holidays were spent with his wife's family. Only once did he take his family to visit his father and stepmother. His strongest memory of that visit was the anger he felt when his stepmother tried talking with him about how much he meant to his father, and how much his father wanted to have a relationship with him—as if there had been something stopping his father from picking up the phone or initiating visits all these years.

When his father was dying, Ned was surprised by how torn he was about whether or not to go see him. His main impulse was to keep the distance that had characterized the relationship over the years. He was struck by the fact that, despite the logic in this stance, he did not feel settled with this choice. He spent long hours talking with his wife. What was the pull? Why should he extend himself when his father had been unwilling to for so many years? Would he feel like he was compromising himself if he were to extend himself to his father now? Yet, would he regret it if he didn't go, when he had this one last chance? In the end, he decided to make the trip. He decided that he would rather live with whatever the visit brought and know that he had made one last try, than live with the question of what might have been.

LORI

Lori's relationship with her partner had ended badly several years earlier amid much deceit and betrayal. They were together for six years, and many of those years had been pretty good ones. But in the end, they fought relentlessly, and parted in anger with little further contact. Having overlapping social circles, they ran into each other periodically, but avoided contact as much as possible. Their conversation was formal and distant.

When Lori learned that Debbie was dying, she was very shaken up. For the first time in a long time, she found herself thinking about the good times that they shared and some of what she had loved about Debbie. With the support of some understanding friends, Lori swallowed her pride and picked up the phone. She was relieved and a little surprised at how receptive Debbie was to her call, and how readily she accepted Lori's suggestion of getting together. While Lori knew she was not prepared to forgive Debbie, she also looked forward to the visit. It would feel good to let the good times have a place again, and to say the goodbye they had never been able to say when this very important relationship had come to an end.

Although Lori and Ned were not in overtly abusive relationships, they had some similar challenges. When confronted by the impending death of a person they had loved, they were forced to look again at what the relationship had and had not been. Each needed to focus on the complexities of the relationship, not only on its negative side. Both of them had to decide what they most wanted for themselves in terms of the last interaction they would have to remember from this important relationship.

Final Lessons

The stories of Carrie, Patrick, Jessie, Lori, and Ned certainly illustrate five very different experiences, yet their responses to those experiences carry some common wisdom that helped them navigate their way, and can help you also. Use the following lessons as basic guidelines for how to say goodbye to a person who has been abusive or neglectful in any way:

YOU NEED TO DO THIS FOR YOURSELF—
NOT TO TAKE CARE OF THE OTHER PERSON

If you can remember, and believe, this, you will be better able to say what you need to as clearly as you can. The old dynamic in an abusive relationship is "If I say it clearly enough, if I do it well enough, then you will love and understand me." There is also the old pull of feeling like you are only important if you are caring for the abusive person by being who they need you to be, or giving them what they want—and you don't want to re-create this dynamic here. If the dying person could never hear you before, they will not necessarily hear or understand you now.

On the other hand, an impending death does change things, and the dying person may respond differently than you would have expected. However, if you enter into the contact with the goal of getting them to respond to you differently, you are at high risk of being disappointed or hurt. You must stay clear on what you need to say. Say what you want and need to—this may be your last chance. And be open to take in what, if anything, is expressed in return.

FOCUS ON THE POSITIVE

How you choose to view the relationship is intimately connected to what you choose to say. Accept the fact that the relationship is a powerful one for you, but take the opportunity to reassign the power to its positive aspects. Remember that much of your ongoing attachment has to do with the positive aspects of the person, not the destructive aspects.

Look at what this person has given you that you value—what about yourself do you like that are characteristics you have because of her or him? Make a list—writing can help you step back and view things more objectively. Also, you can return to something you've written, and review and revise it when your feelings change.

WHEN TALKING ABOUT PAST HARM,
KEEP TO SIMPLE, DIRECT STATEMENTS LIKE:

> *"In so many ways, our relationship has been hard, but I want you to know that . . ."*
>
> *"It's been a while since we have been in contact, but you are important to me, and . . ."*
>
> *"I think you know how painful our family life was for all of us . . ."*
>
> *"Life was rough in the family when I was a kid . . ."*
>
> *"We were a pretty unhappy family, but I want you to know . . ."*
>
> *"Alcohol [or violence, or whatever it was] was a major part of our family life, but I want you to know some of the other things I got from the family [or you] as well . . ."*

If the relationship was abusive in some ways, these may seem like gross understatements, but they at least provide a way to frame the relationship history with some honesty while you focus on the aspects of the relationship that are of value to you. Unless there is a clear *mutual* desire to look back and talk about a problematic past, keep end-of-life discussions focused on the parts of the past you want to keep with you, and on the present.

AN "I'M SORRY" NEAR DEATH

Use an "I'm sorry" from the dying person as a statement of recognition and validation of the reality and pain you experienced for so long. An apology near death does not mean you have to forgive the person for all past harm, nor does it mean you have to feel it sets everything right. Also, know that while an apology can feel confusing at the time of death, it is something you will always have. It will probably become more important over time as you continue to grow and further develop your understanding of yourself and of the relationship.

REDEFINE THE RELATIONSHIP

There are ways you can do this with a dying person, ways that may not have felt possible before. The interaction at this point is not about continuing the relationship in the old form; the form that continues to have such a strong pull. It is also not about trying to rework an ongoing interaction. *It is about* looking at what you want to claim for yourself from the relationship while the person is still alive.

The fear of getting pulled into that abusive dynamic may diminish for two reasons: first because the reality of an impending death often changes the idea that this relationship can develop into something, and second because the old patterns won't be forever ongoing. Simply knowing this person is dying may give you some freedom to interact with them in ways that did not seem doable before.

Questions to Answer

Use the following list of questions to help you sort through some of your feelings. Remember that these questions probably do not have easy answers. Your answers may change from one time to the next. And again, it might be helpful to write your thoughts and feelings down, both to get them out in words, and to be able to go back over them as you rethink what you want to say, or do.

WHAT IS IT I WISH TO SAY?

Spend time on this one. Think about it, write it down, talk with someone you trust. Thinking about what you wish to say does not mean you'll have to say it.

WHAT DO I FEAR THAT WOULD KEEP ME FROM SAYING WHAT I WANT TO?

Usually, your fears are exaggerated because you have lived for so long with "imagining" what might happen, instead of the reality of the other person's response to your actions. Their response is likely to be much less dramatic than what you imagine. One way to be prepared is to ask yourself, "What would be the worst that could happen if I do/say what I wish to?"

WHAT MIGHT I REGRET IF I DON'T TAKE THE OPPORTUNITY NOW?

Think about the future without this person, and think about how you would like to leave the relationship, with or without their help.

WHAT SUPPORTS DO I NEED IN ORDER TO AVOID
GETTING PULLED INTO OLD PATTERNS?
Talk with people you are close to—friends, a therapist, another family member—who can help you hold on to your
newer, adult reality of the relationship.

WHAT FORMAT WILL BEST ACHIEVE MY GOALS?
Face-to-face—It may be that sitting down with someone face-
to-face, which has a greater sense of intimacy and understanding and allows for an exchange, is what you are looking for. In
this exchange, you also communicate beyond or in addition to
words with your body language, facial expressions, and tone of
voice.

Phone call—Calls allow an interaction, but do not have the
intimacy of face-to-face. With calls you can stay focused on
the words because you don't have the interference of body language, or of facial expressions.

A letter—Letters offer a safe interaction; one where you
don't need to fear you will lose what you are trying to say.
With a letter you can state what you want, without the risk of
getting pulled into a dialogue. You can read it over and edit it
until you feel it expresses what you want to say.

WHAT ABOUT SILENCE? NOT TALKING AT ALL?
If you keep yourself silent because you are afraid you won't be
heard, or fear the other person won't want what you offer, you
may be left with regrets about what you wanted to do, but
didn't; wanted to say, but didn't. Or you may decide that what
you want to say won't be tolerated, so you choose to use your

other support systems to talk about the reality of this relationship, and you connect with the dying person in other ways. Patrick chose to be involved through actions. He did not deny his own experience; he did that piece—talking it through—with other people.

There is no single, right way to bring closure to a destructive relationship. How you go about it, what you say, do, or don't say will be a very personal decision, influenced by many factors. You may choose to see the person, or even be involved in their care. You may choose to keep your distance, and say what you need to in letters or phone calls. You may even choose to have no contact at all. The important thing is that you make your choices consciously.

SIX

Helping Children Say Goodbye

*I knew she was real sick, but I didn't really think she would die.
No one said anything about it, and I kind of thought it,
but I never asked—I think I was afraid of what the answer would be.
Now I wish I had asked. I keep thinking that I would have done
some things differently if I had known. Now it's too late.*
—MARK, AGE TWELVE,
FOUR DAYS AFTER HIS MOTHER'S DEATH

On Saturday morning, each of the children arrived for the support group, bringing their favorite tape or CD, as they had agreed to do the week before. The topic of music had come up during last week's discussion about coping with difficult feelings when a parent is sick. The group was made up of boys and girls, ages nine through twelve, all of whom had a parent with cancer. At this time, several of their parents were doing very poorly. The children, however, were talkative, animated, and silly, as usual. On this day, each child was going to have the opportunity to play their favorite song for the group. Twelve-year-old Olivia waited impatiently for her turn. When she played her song, she sat quietly, tapping her foot and moving her shoulders to the beat, until it came to her favorite line and she sang along loudly, "I'm dying inside and nobody knows but me."

We like to believe that childhood is a time of innocence, and that it is rare for children to have to cope with such weighty issues as death. The reality is that many, many children experience the loss of someone important to them by the time they finish high school. Parents, grandparents, friends, friends' parents, or teachers may die. For children, as with adults, there is no way around the pain that death will cause. Yet, in efforts to protect them, we so often leave our children emotionally alone to cope with their losses.

What gets in the way of helping children cope with very difficult and unavoidable experiences of life? In large part, our discomfort addressing our own difficult feelings makes talking about death, especially with children, very difficult. Also, our tendency to underestimate their ability to understand. And we have a strong wish to protect children from pain. While this wish is normal and healthy, it's *very* important that we hold ourselves back from acting on it. We can't protect our children from pain. There are always disappointments and losses in life.

What we can do for our children, however, is teach them the tools they need to deal with the painful events that life hands them. We can help children know they are not alone to cope with pain, and teach them ways to understand and manage their feelings, use others for support, and *believe* they can manage the difficulties they encounter. These are the extremely important gifts that we can give our children.

Children Sense the Emotional Climate

Children are very perceptive, and no matter what age, they learn far more from what you do, than from what you say. Did you ever notice that, although every child is unique, and every parent is unique, every child knows *exactly* how to provoke his or her parent? Or that when you are the most preoccupied, stressed, or tired, is exactly when your young child needs your full attention? Why is that? Basically, because children and parents know each other quite well. And children are very responsive to the emotional climate around them. Even children who are far too young to understand what is going on will know when something upsetting is happening. When the death of someone you love is likely, you will be in pain, and your child will know it.

EMILY

Emily was nine and had just begun fourth grade when they learned that her mother had cancer. It had been a rough year with hospitalizations, endless doctor visits, and medical treatments that sometimes seemed worse than the illness itself. Her mother was not responding well to treatment and the cancer was progressing. Over the last month, she was noticeably sicker, thinner, and weaker. She spent much of her time in bed, sleeping.

The day of Emily's school concert was a particularly bad one for her mother. She was nauseated, sometimes confused, and in pain—the medications weren't helping as well as they did some days. Emily knew as soon as she came home from school that it wasn't a good day. Her father was home, and he looked worried.

"Is Mom going to be able to come tonight?" she asked him.

"I don't think so, she hasn't been feeling very well, but maybe she'll be better after she naps." Emily was scared, but mostly, right now she felt angry. There were so many things this year that her mother hadn't attended. Tonight, she and four classmates had a part in one song that they sang by themselves, and her mother was going to miss it. All the other kids would have their mothers there. She slammed the door behind her on the way into her bedroom. She wasn't going to be nice and quiet just because her mother was sleeping. Her father came in after her, obviously cross.

"What are you doing? You know your mother is trying to sleep."

"I don't care! If she cared about me, she'd come tonight."

Seeing Emily's eyes filling up with tears was more than her father could bear. How could this be happening? It was so unfair. She should be able to happily go off to her concert tonight, secure in the knowledge that her parents were watching her. What's more, as bad as things were, he knew they were going to get worse. He was trying his best to keep things as normal as possible at home, but it wasn't working very well.

Exhausted and irritable, he tried to convince Emily that this one concert was not such a big deal so that she wouldn't feel so bad. He also tried to minimize the seriousness of her mother's condition, believing that this would help her feel better, at least for now, and put off the pain until a later date. As she sat there, quiet and glaring at him, he felt increasingly angry at his helplessness. Not being able to think of anything more to say, he left the room. Emily was left alone.

Communication is not based only on the specific things you say, but rather on your subtle nuances—tone of voice, facial expressions, body movement, tension, choice of wording. So when you say, "Mom is fine," but your eyes look very sad, or you turn away quickly and change the subject as Emily's father did, a child will know that you are lying. The message, then, is not that things truly are fine, but that you, and the child, must pretend. Or that something is so bad that you must lie about it. All children have experience in lying, and they know it when they see it.

Children and adolescents (despite what they might like to believe) are very dependent on the adults in their life and the people they love. If someone close to them is sick, they, like the adults around them, will be worried about that person, and, by extension, themselves. They will wonder, "How will this illness or death affect my life?" "How will it make me different than my friends?" "Who will be there for me?"

Helping Our Children Manage the Pain

Our job is to guide children through their early years, so by the time they reach adulthood, they are able to negotiate the world independently. In a sense, how well your children achieve this is the measure of your own success. We all want to do well on our parenting report cards. We generally are graded (if only in our minds) on the degree to which our children are achieving the goals we expect.

If you have as a goal that your child will be protected from pain, you get an A if she seems to be without pain, and anywhere from a C to an F if she is clearly hurting. If your child is upset about a serious illness, in addition to feeling bad for her, you may feel that you are failing her. Since there is no way to make important losses insignificant or not painful, the most you can accomplish toward this goal is teaching your child that the pain she feels must not show.

If, on the other hand, your goal is helping your child *man-*

age the pain she feels, or helping her know she does not have to manage her pain alone, your actions and responses will automatically be very different. Now you get an A if your child turns to you or others for support, and learns ways to express and manage her difficult feelings in acceptable ways, and an F if she is acting out her feelings in ways that could harm her or others.

Remember that you don't need to fix anything—and you can't. Imagine how different her father's response would have been if he reacted, not from the belief that he should minimize Emily's pain, or shield her from it, but from a belief that he could help her cope with the pain. The simple response of saying, "I know you're upset. I'm sorry this feels so bad," and sitting down quietly with a child is an invitation to that child to lean on you; you've let her know you're there for her. The acts or words that convey to a child that you understand how she feels help both of you feel less alone and helpless.

Talk with the child about what they are able to do. What, realistically, is within Emily's power to do to manage this situation? Her mother can't be at the concert, but maybe wearing a necklace of hers, or keeping something of her mother's in her pocket, can be a reminder to Emily that her mother is with her in spirit, and will be thinking of her. Maybe Emily would like to include her mother in some way, like singing the song for her before she goes, or having Dad tape record or videotape the concert for Mom to listen to later. Children are wonderfully creative in devising solutions for managing problems, especially when supported and encouraged to do so. Both you and your child have the opportunity to feel better about a bad situation.

From this viewpoint, you can take comfort in knowing that your hurting child can turn to you and, if you listen, let you know what she needs. You can take pride in her growing ability to manage difficult situations and emotions. You can, then, truly be there for her, to dry her tears, give her the extra hug, or the special attention she needs. You can protect her from having to manage some of life's most troubling experiences alone.

Perfection Is Not the Goal

This is not to say that parents and other adults need to be perfect. Of course there are times when a parent is too tired or upset themselves to deal with one more tantrum or struggle. And there are plenty of times when a parent is in too much pain to be able to tolerate tears or questions from their children. It is important to remember that no single interaction is tremendously significant. Nor are several intermittent interactions. Rather, it is the overall message and belief system, and the ways in which these get communicated over time that really carry weight.

It's fine to tell a child, "I can't talk about this now." It's the truth. But go back to it at a time when you can. In that way, you've let your child know that you've heard her, you remember, and you're available to be there for her, but not on exactly the time clock she has chosen. What's more, you've modeled self-care and setting limits, which is something children need to learn to do for themselves as they grow. You may know that it is going to be a long time before you're ready to openly address very painful feelings about the death of the person you and your child love. Help find another adult for your child to talk to—an aunt, a friend, a counselor. Let her know that you support the idea of her talking to a trusted adult, and that you recognize the strength and courage it takes to face and express feelings.

The Need to Tell the Truth

I learned long ago, as a pediatric nurse, the importance of never lying to children. Working with children who had cancer, I was often in the position of helping a child through painful medical procedures. Tempting as it was to tell a child ahead of time, "This won't hurt," in order to alleviate his anticipatory fear or to gain his cooperation, this would work only once. From the moment that child felt pain after I had told him there wouldn't be any, I could no longer gain his trust. As a result, I had not only lost my ability to comfort him for any future painful procedures, I also had no ability to comfort him when he was facing a procedure that was truly not painful. My words had proven meaningless before, so he couldn't easily trust me again.

I quickly learned that if I said to a child, "This will hurt, but I'll be here to help you," I could support him by preparing him, or help soothe him during and after the procedure. I was an ally: I told the truth and had proven that I could be trusted. I could tolerate his pain and believed he could, too. In the future, when he was frightened about a procedure that would not cause pain, I could actually help by allaying his fears. When I said, "Don't worry, this won't hurt," he could relax. Trust and tolerance go a long way.

The same holds true for emotional pain. You can provide comfort and support to a scared or upset child only when he or she trusts you. When a child asks if a very sick parent is going to be okay, the temptation is often to try to minimize, or flat out lie about a very bad prognosis. In the moment, it can seem like it will help the child feel better. In the moment, it may even make you feel better. The problem is this—the child usually knows you are being less than honest. Even if you succeed in fooling him for the time being, it is likely that he will learn you weren't telling the truth. You will lose *all* ability to comfort him. What you risk is that in the future, he will perceive any of your reassurances, no matter how truthful, as empty words.

JENNIFER

Jennifer's mother was very sick from metastatic breast cancer, and wasn't responding well to treatment. At the recommendation of her oncology nurse, Jennifer's mother called me for assistance in helping support her daughter as she fought her illness. Jennifer, age six, knew that her mother had cancer and had been encouraged to ask questions. She had been told about chemotherapy and radiation. She had also been encouraged to talk about the fears she had about "something happening to Mommy." She never used the word "die," but her play showed a particular interest in things related to death.

At one point, when her mother was hospitalized for a medical crisis, Jennifer asked me, "Is my mommy going to be okay?" I was well aware of my urge to tell her, "Yes, of course," but swallowed it. We sat and talked for a while. I told her that we were all very worried, her mom was very, very sick, that the doctors were doing their best, and we were hoping very hard that she would be able to come home again.

"Me too," she cried, "I miss my mommy sooo much!" She cuddled up to

me and we sat in silence for a few minutes. Then she jumped up. "I'm going to make Mommy a card that will make her happy. She thinks I'm a special artist, you know." Jennifer got out her supplies and worked diligently, decorating a get well card. I don't think I've ever seen more stickers and glitter on a card than there was on that one. She then carefully put it in an envelope, sealed it, and placed it where her dad would remember to take it to the hospital that evening.

Jennifer's mother did make it through that crisis. She came home and had an extended period of feeling well. At a later time, her mother was hospitalized for a brief treatment. I saw Jennifer during that time and again she asked me if her mom would be coming home. This time, I could confidently tell her that yes, her mom would be home the next day. She then went on with her play. Because I had not tried to fool her the last time, she could believe me this time.

Reactions to Death at Different Ages

Death is a difficult topic to talk about because it is tough to comprehend, even for adults. It's tough to imagine not existing in the form we know. The concept of "forever" is equally hard to grasp. There are many, many questions surrounding death that most of us answer based on our long-held beliefs, and faith; not based on facts. The only fact we have is that we will die.

What happens after death? Does the soul go on? To where, and in what way? What about heaven and hell? Children ask all these same questions. As perplexing as these questions are for us to answer to adults, when we are talking with children, the answer can seem even more confusing, given our uncertainty about what the child can understand. We often worry that all of the unknowns about death, as well as the idea of burying a body in the ground, or cremating a body, will frighten children.

Yet, I have *never* known a child to become more frightened by factual information than by their own imaginings. And children are perceptive. If you've avoided or sidestepped giving your child an answer to her questions, she knows it, and might in fact think the answer is clearly too awful to talk about. You need to provide an environment in which your child can ask *any* question, and express her fears. This gives you the opportunity to know and correct any of her false, and likely scary, imaginings.

It's helpful to have some guidelines about the ways in which children typically view death at different ages, and the kinds of questions they might be asking you about a death, or about dying in general. View the following guidelines as loose—children vary tremendously in the concepts they grasp. What one child understands at age four, another will only begin to understand at age six. Knowledge of cognitive development is *only* a helpful starting point—you then need to listen carefully, over time, to the questions your child asks, and you need to be aware of how she is behaving. Notice the way your child *makes sense* of the information you give her. This is the best way to understand the needs of any child.

EARLY YEARS

Infants and toddlers are not able to anticipate events, but will experience and react to events as they occur around them.

Babies will react to the absence of someone they love, and to any emotional changes in their environments. Once a child is mobile, you may see them search for the person who is absent. Expect a very young child to be fussier, more clingy, and to regress to earlier behavior when things are stressful. While it isn't possible to explain an impending death to a preverbal child in a way that will entirely make sense to them, it is important to keep things as consistent as possible for them.

Once a child has started developing language, give simple, straightforward explanations. "Mommy died. She can't come back." "Mommy was sad to leave you, she didn't want to." The child may not be able to grasp the concept, but she will feel attended to, and you will build on her understanding as she matures.

PRESCHOOL YEARS

Preschool-age children are just beginning to get curious about death, and starting to ask questions. They think very concretely at this age, and see things as existing only from their own perspective. They see death around them—a dead squirrel or bird, a pet, or a person they know—and although they can't contemplate the abstract concepts involved, they clearly have a sense of there being something different and significant about death.

I will never forget when a little three-and-a-half-year-old girl I knew began asking questions about death. She engaged in the type of "conversation" that is typical of her age, where she directed her questions at someone, but then answered them herself. Out of the blue one day, while Laura was coloring, she asked her mother, "What happens to people's clothes when they die, do they get blood on them?" Surprised, her mother hadn't quite thought of an answer when Laura answered, "No, I don't think so." She then continued on. "When people die, why do we bury them in cemeteries?" Again, she quickly answered herself, "I know. If we left them on the sidewalk, we would trip on them." Finally, after a minute, she asked her last question. "But how do they get to the cemeteries? Oh, I know. Their wheelchairs drop them off." In this way, so typical of a young child, she was trying to put together the world she saw around her with the notions she had encountered about death.

Important, young children below the age of five to seven or so don't understand the concept of time. The idea of tomorrow, two weeks, or two years away is all the same. There is only now and not now. Along with this, they also don't have an understanding of a linear progression of time. Hence, you often hear children say things like, "When I'm big and you're little . . ." when talking to an adult, or "When I'm bigger than you . . ." Without an understanding of time and irreversibility, you can't understand permanence, or the concept of forever.

So death, like everything else, can only be understood in the present. Children understand that someone is missing or gone from their present experience, but no matter how well you explain it, they will not fully be able to grasp the idea that when someone dies, they will remain gone always. Because of this, don't be surprised when your child seems to understand your simple and clear explanation, but then needs it explained over and over again.

Much of the literature describes school age as the time when children begin asking spiritual questions—questions about the difference between body and soul. It seems to me, though, that they often start asking these questions much earlier. I remember when my own son was just over three years old, and we drove past a cemetery. He asked about how people can be buried after they die and also go to heaven. I stumbled through an explanation the best I could at the time. I told him that after we die, our bodies stop working and don't do anything anymore; they can't see, eat, play, talk, or think. But our soul, the part of us that we can't see but that is the special part of us, that thinks and feels and makes us who we are, goes to heaven. His eyes got very big. "What if it wouldn't *want* to go without your body? What if it would be *scared?*" In his very concrete way, he too was trying to understand the physical world that he knew along with this new idea. While he couldn't yet grasp the concept, he was beginning to wonder.

Young children also experience what is called "magical thinking." They believe that they cause things to happen by their thoughts and wishes. If the parent of a three- or four-year-old gets very sick, that child will often feel responsible, attributing the illness to anger she felt toward the parent, or behavior she believed was bad. Because of this, it is extremely important to tell young children, repeatedly, that it was nothing *they* did that made the person sick. Thoughts don't make things happen.

Even very young children are responsive to the emotional climate around them. When a parent or grandparent is very ill, young children will sense the tension and worries of others, and will often respond to these circumstances by becoming more clingy, whiny, and demanding. They may resume wetting the bed, or even having accidents in the daytime. While these behavioral changes can be very draining to cope with, it is important to remember that they are normal under the circumstances. They are not signs of burgeoning psychological problems. They are signs that the child, like the adults around her, is upset, worried, and feeling insecure. With support, understanding, and time, these behaviors will disappear.

SCHOOL AGE

By the time children are school age—five, six, or seven—they develop an understanding of the concept of permanence. They can understand death as something that is irreversible. When someone is dead, they are dead forever, and will not return to life. Not only can they understand the concept of physical death; in many ways, they are fascinated by it. A dead animal is a sight that inspires curiosity. The dead bird they bury one day, they will dig up again several days later to inspect. Mary, a seven-year-old girl I knew, found a dead mouse in her backyard. She, her friend, and her five-year-old sister, staged a funeral and buried the mouse in a shoebox. Two days later, curiosity got the better of them and they dug the mouse up to see what it was like after burial. To their horror and apparent delight, the mouse was crawling with maggots. After screaming, they set about poking the mouse with a stick, and rolling it back and forth some, to see the animal from all sides. The idea of the worms fascinated them as they studied the decomposition of the body. Needless to say, there was much speculation about the same thing happening to humans.

School-age children are intrigued by reasons and rules. Watch elementary school children play—they love games with rules. Even imaginative play gets infused with rules.

Children this age like life to be reasonable and logical, and they apply this same way of thinking to illness and death. They want to figure out all the "whys"—the reasons that things happen, the rules about death. At this age, they begin asking more in-depth spiritual questions, since they can more fully understand the concept of physical death.

School-age children tend to be very focused on the ways in which a death will impact them in the future. Who will help with homework, make the special birthday cake, cheer for them at the baseball game? It is very normal for a child to be far more worried that Grandma—who is getting sicker and may die next week—will ruin their birthday party next Saturday than to focus more generally on the larger meaning the death will hold in their lives.

When school-age children are coping with a serious illness, an impending death, or a death that has happened, they will feel mixtures of anger and sadness, as do adults. They often feel guilty too, due to some feelings of responsibility for the illness or death—even when this has no basis in fact.

They will probably remember bad behaviors, or angry feelings they had toward the person, and feel responsible to a degree, equating these past events in some way with the current illness or death: This is the magical thinking I mentioned earlier. By this age, children no longer cognitively see themselves as all-powerful or as the center of the world, but around death these feelings creep back in.

One nine-year-old girl I worked with, Karen, confessed after several sessions that she thought her father had died because she had made him so angry the prior week when she had been defiant about helping with the yard work. Not only was she worried that she had contributed to his death, but she was also afraid that her mother would be furious with her if she knew just how obstinate Karen had been. Just putting this fear into words was a relief for Karen. I talked with her briefly about how typical it is for people to feel responsible when someone they love dies, but that it wasn't her fault. While words don't completely relieve the irrational aspect of guilt, she clearly relaxed, and was able to partially let go of this emotional burden.

When I hear children talk about their experiences of serious illness in their family, they often express jealously about the amount of attention focused on the sick person, and resentment about feeling overlooked or ignored. When school-age children are trying to cope with an illness or death, they will often have a difficult time concentrating on routine tasks or schoolwork. This can become a source of struggle between them and their caretakers, especially if the adults (teachers included) don't understand or recognize the root of the problem. This is simply that their overwhelming feelings get channeled into their behavior, and they act out much more.

PREADOLESCENT

Preadolescent children, like younger children, also experience an array of feelings, but since their development is more advanced, they often have a greater understanding of what death means. They also have a good understanding of the difference between a body and a spirit, and in keeping with their love of explanations and reason, you can expect them to focus on bodily issues. They are often interested in the gruesome aspect of death. To them, blood and guts are quite fascinating. When someone they know dies, preadolescents will want all of the details about what happened to the body. This is particularly true if the person died in a violent way, or the death resulted in altering the body in some way—such as a really devastating cancer.

Because of this fascination, children at this age are likely to ask *a lot* of questions. Expect very specific questions about the appearance of the body, such as how bloody the death scene was, the color of the person's skin after he died, whether his eyes or mouth were open. An eleven-year-old I worked with started asking questions months after his father had been buried, and was particularly curious about the likely condition of the body after months in the ground. He wondered if there would still be any skin. Another child had questions about the amount of blood in the bed of a grandparent whose death had involved hemorrhaging.

The idea of giving these kinds of details can seem very morbid to you, and you may worry that they will be frightening for the child. But remember, children have very vivid imaginations. If a child who is asking you questions, and expecting answers, gets the message from you that the description of the death is too horrible for you to even talk about, the images he or she will conjure up will be *at least* as bad as the reality, and probably much worse.

TEENAGERS

Adolescents develop the ability to fully grasp abstract concepts. They are, like adults, able to conceptualize about different spiritual concepts, an afterlife, or the idea of transformation from one realm to another (life to death). They understand death as universal, and know that it happens to all living things. They don't, however, entirely generalize this concept, and have difficulty fully including themselves or peers in this inevitability. Although they could tell you that death comes to everyone, they live with a sense of personal invulnerability and immortality. Look at the risky behavior of many teens!

Children outgrow magical thinking by school age, but it seems to reemerge in ways, even in adolescence when teens have to deal with the death of a person they are very close to. They will struggle with feelings of responsibility—that the stress they caused contributed to the person's illness, or that they are paying for having wished, in times of anger, that the person was out of their life.

When death does touch the lives of teenagers, they will generally be thrown by feelings of helplessness and lack of control. Their sense that life goes on forever and their unrealistic sense of power has been upset. Feeling out of control is particularly difficult at this age, because feelings of self-sufficiency and independence are so important. Most teens like to believe they no longer need to be told what to do, and feel they are perfectly capable of taking care of themselves.

Without being aware of it, they depend upon the stability and security provided by their caregivers, which enables them to try out new levels of independence and peer involvement. When that security is threatened by serious illness or death, it is very scary. Adolescents will feel a need to retreat to dependence on others they love and trust. This is acutely difficult, as it flies directly in the face of what they are trying to accomplish developmentally: independence.

The question "Who will take care of me?" is paramount for all children, and they will benefit—at any age—from repeated reassurances. When one of the people they depend on for their care is seriously ill or dying, or when an impending death is seriously affecting their caretakers, reassure them that, although this is extremely difficult and everyone feels bad, they are safe, and you will care for them.

Once youngsters reach the teenage years, the complex emotional experience of preadolescence is made even more tumultuous by their physical and hormonal changes. As they become more independent, they struggle in new ways to define who they are as individuals. Peers become extremely important.

We all know that teenagers want to be like their peers. Teens often feel very different from their friends because of a crisis in their family. Their friends are focused on school stuff, relationships, break-ups, struggles with parents, and other day-to-day dramas. An adolescent coping with the serious illness and death of someone she loves feels different at this time when sameness is of utmost importance. She will work very hard to mask this difference between herself and her peers.

I first met Brittany about six months before her mother's death. At fourteen, Brittany was very involved in the care of her mother. She went straight home from school most days, not because she was told she had to, but because she wanted to. Usually, she did her homework in her mother's room so she would be there if her mother needed anything, and she worked hard at keeping her grades up, and staying involved with activities. Brittany continued to spend plenty of time in the evening on the phone with her friends, but this presented her with a problem. She wanted to be like her friends, but inside she didn't feel like them. When I talked with her, she admitted to resenting her friends sometimes, for worrying so much about things that she now considered unimportant. She also said she felt angry when they complained about their parents. At least they had parents! It wasn't going to be long before she no longer had a mother. She felt like she would happily face every fight she and her mother had ever had, if only her mother wouldn't die. Still, she never said much to any of her friends about her feelings, believing that they wouldn't want to hear it.

Also, it's easy (and maybe even necessary) to fight with your parents, and even hate them at times, *unless* they are going to die. A possible death puts a whole new perspective on things. Suddenly, nothing is the same anymore, and teens not only hide this reality from their friends, they may even hide it from themselves. They will work very hard to keep life as normal as possible.

On occasion, usually when a death is imminent, I see adolescents in my practice who want to talk about their struggles and the changes in their families. These tend to be kids who want help convincing a parent of something, such as being allowed to be at home and miss school when the death is near, or being awakened during the night if the person dies. More often, teenagers have no interest in talking to a strange adult about such important and personal experiences.

It is important to let adolescents make their own decisions about how to be involved in a death—don't try and force an adolescent to do something he doesn't want to. There's little that a person can control surrounding death, and it's important to have choices where it is possible. If there is a way to get adolescents together who have had similar life experiences around loss, do so. Perhaps a schoolmate or friend from the neighborhood has experienced a death and will be able to understand and sympathize. This approach is often the most helpful. Invite questions often. When they want to, they will ask.

Listening to Children

The most important way to know what children understand, and how they think, is to listen to them. Use the idea of listening very broadly. Listen to what they say, and listen to what they communicate in other ways—through their gestures, their play, and their interactions with others. Children of all ages, but young children especially, often can't tell you what they feel. They haven't yet learned to pay attention to, or label different feelings. But they will be able to communicate their feelings to you in ways other than words, and it can be helpful to them for you to label what you see them expressing. For example, if a child is irritable and uncooperative, tell him you know that he is angry, or you know that he is sad—whatever seems to most accurately describe what you are seeing.

BILLY
I met eleven-year-old Billy several months before his mother died. She had a degenerative illness and was expected to die within a month or two. His father could not bring himself to tell Billy that she was dying, and couldn't

quite believe that he should be told. Their hospice nurse recommended that he call me, and ask me to meet with Billy. Before I met with Billy, his father and I agreed that I wouldn't go out of my way to give specific information about how sick and near death his mother was, but that I would be truthful about any questions he asked. At that point, his mother was confined to bed, no longer able to do any self-care, was often confused, and sometimes nonresponsive.

After talking about a variety of things, Billy confided to me that sometimes he worried his mother would die.

"You know there's nothing that can be done to help her improve, and that everyone is working to help her stay comfortable?" I replied.

"Yes, I know." We talked about the ways she had changed over the past month. He talked about his thoughts that other people, including himself, could die. But it was clear that this was as far as he wanted to go. He spent much of the time talking about other things—activities he was involved in, sports, friends, and school.

During subsequent visits, he talked some about what it was like for him to no longer have his mother participating in his activities—not watching his baseball games, not driving him to friends' houses, and, important, not having planned a birthday party for him several weeks earlier. It was not until our fourth visit that Billy looked at me, and asked directly, "Is my mother going to die?"

"Yes, she is," I told him.

"I know," he said very quietly, eyes downcast. "I don't want her to die."

It was not until that moment that Billy wanted to hear those words, and that is when he asked. Although I questioned, and gave Billy many invitations to talk about his mother's death, it was important for me to go at his pace, and offer a listening ear as he focused on all the changes, losses, and impending loss in his life. We were fortunate, because we had the time to go at the pace he needed to, which is often the case with long-term illness. Sometimes, however, someone with a long-term illness may die much more quickly than you expect, and you may not have had the time to discuss the certainty of their death—either with them, or with your child. But, as long as you've been honest with your child about the illness being serious, you've laid the groundwork to continue to support him as he copes with this unexpected loss.

Keep the following in mind when you "listen" to your child:

WHILE ADULTS ARE BUSY TRYING TO PROTECT CHILDREN, CHILDREN OFTEN TRY TO PROTECT ADULTS

Children won't ask questions they think will upset you. They don't like to feel helpless, so won't ask questions that might make a parent cry, unless they are invited or encouraged to do so. Children will often avoid asking questions that they fear the answer to, almost as if putting the question into words will make the fear come true; as if not talking about fears will ward off the reality.

OFFER CHILDREN SIMPLE EXPLANATIONS, AND LISTEN TO THEIR RESPONSES

Say something simple like "Grandma is very sick. The doctors can't do anything more to make her well again. We can all help her stay as comfortable as possible." Then wait. Children will usually let you know if they want more information. They may ask questions about the illness, they might ask directly, "Will Grandma die?" (If you think the death is imminent, say this, rather than wait.)

ANSWER ANY QUESTIONS AS HONESTLY AND SIMPLY AS YOU CAN

It's fine to say, "I don't know" if it's the truth. If you do answer, "I don't know" to questions about death, and what happens after death, ask your child what she thinks. This can give you a lot of information about her level of understanding. It will also give you the opportunity to clear up any misconceptions she might have. Your child may not have any other questions initially. However, you've let her know she can talk about the sickness and eventual death. She will come back to it when she's ready. If she doesn't ask again on her own, invite discussion again soon.

CHILDREN CAN ONLY TOLERATE STRONG, DIFFICULT EMOTIONS FOR SHORT PERIODS

When children indicate they've had enough, by changing the subject to something very different, getting silly, trying to leave, or getting very fidgety, let the conversation stop. Then they need to go on to other things.

Finally, when listening to children, remember that many of the painful feelings they express are normal, not signs of emotional problems. The most common concerns I hear expressed by parents when there is an impending or recent death in the family is that their child seems angry or very sad. Of course a child feels these things, who wouldn't? Feelings, in and of themselves, are not problems—they are normal human reactions to loss, and need attention and room for expression. It is behaviors, or ways that these feelings do or do not get expressed, that can be a problem.

If your child is expressing intense feelings in ways that let the feelings be known, but are not harmful to him or others, great. Help your child know that his feelings are normal, and help him find ways to work with them. Let him know that you also feel angry or sad about the death.

If, on the other hand, your child is expressing feelings in a way that is harmful or dangerous, it *is* a problem. A child who is withdrawing significantly from family, friends, or activities, fighting with peers, or engaging in risk-taking or destructive behavior, such as drug or alcohol use, is letting you know that he is having trouble managing his difficult feelings. In such cases, don't hesitate to get professional help for you and your child.

Explaining What It Means "to Die"

When you talk with children about what it means to die, use simple, direct, and honest language. Giving in to the temptation to "soften" harsh concepts usually backfires. Euphemisms are very confusing; avoid them at all costs. Say what you mean. If you say that Grandma will be "going to sleep forever," going to sleep at night sounds like a very uninviting idea, and your child may respond by being afraid to go to bed and to fall asleep. To say that someone is going to "leave us," makes it sound, at least in part, voluntary, the way most leave-takings are. This will often leave a child feeling a threat of abandonment, and also anger—why would someone she loves and depends on leave her? Don't they know the child needs them? Don't they care? Other common euphemisms for death, such as "pass," "pass on," or "lost," are equally as confusing.

Use the words "die" and "death." Then you can share what you know and believe, as well as ask your child what she thinks. For young children and school-age children, you can explain physical death in terms of the body stopping working. "When Grandpa dies, his heart will stop beating," or "When we die, our hearts stop beating, and we stop breathing." Children can feel their own breath, and can feel their own hearts beating as you discuss it. Describe how these slow down, and eventually stop when a person dies. This is very different from sleep, which we do to keep our bodies healthy and strong. A person who is dead looks peaceful, the way a person who is sleeping looks peaceful, but in all other ways, the two are different.

Explaining Spiritual Beliefs

Beliefs about the separation of body and spirit, and the continuation of the spirit, can feel difficult to explain to children. Virginia Fry, author of *Part of Me Died Too*, offers a very helpful way to describe these abstract concepts. She uses the analogy of a hand in a glove being like the spirit in the body, with the spirit slipping into the body at birth the way a hand goes into a glove. Then when the body is ready to die, the spirit slips out again, leaving the limp glove empty. This type of analogy can be modified to fit your religious and spiritual beliefs about death. In the Resources section, I have recommended a number of excellent books about death written for children of different ages.

Religious beliefs about an afterlife can be comforting to a child, and offer him the idea that his loved one will still be with him, but in a different form after death. It is important, however, to avoid trying to entirely take away the child's pain through explanations of an afterlife. For example, stressing the belief that Mom or Grandpa will still be present, or watching over him as soon as he expresses sadness about a loss, suggests to him that there aren't good grounds for his feelings. If Dad is "still here," why does your child miss him so much? Your child will learn to keep his sad feelings to himself.

Don't try to convince a child of things you don't believe, or aren't sure of yourself. Trying to offer, as fact, religious convictions or explanations that you don't entirely believe isn't usually helpful. Talk about what you believe, and let your child know what questions you have, then encourage him to talk about what he believes and ask his questions. This will open the door for ongoing discussions, and offer far more comfort than will platitudes.

Often adults are afraid to discuss painful issues with children for fear of crying in front of them. Not only is it okay to cry in front of your child, it can offer him a good example of a way in which he can express his strong feelings. It can also be a good opportunity to talk about feelings with him. It is very important, however, to let him know that he is not responsible for taking care of you, that you will be all right, you are just sad and can tolerate crying.

Use simple statements like "I'm sad because I'm going to

miss Grandma. Sometimes it helps me feel better to cry. I know you are sad, too. I bet you feel like crying sometimes." In this way, you let your child know honestly how you feel, you show him that it's okay to express feelings, and you assure him that you, and he, will be all right. Painful feelings are just that. There is nothing threatening or unsafe about crying.

Involve Children in Caregiving

Don't wait until your children ask to be included in illness or death-related events in the family. Invite them to join in. When asked by parents to meet with children, I usually try to have some time to talk with everyone involved together and then some time with the child or children alone. In this way, I learn a little about the family, but more important, the children are able to get a sense of me.

After talking with children about their questions and concerns, I always ask how I can be helpful to them, what they would like me to communicate to their parents or caretakers about all we have discussed. Almost without fail, they want me to convince their caretakers to include them in the events to come. They often ask to stay at home on days when death seems imminent, be called home immediately if the death occurs when they are at school or a friend's house, or awakened during the night if the death happens then. And they usually want to go to the wake and funeral. I have heard these requests from children as young as five.

I remember working with three-year-old Sarah, and her mother, Eileen. Sarah and her mother had always spent much of their time at her grandmother's house. Although Sarah was too young to understand what was happening, she knew something was different at Grandmother's. Now when they went over to visit, her grandmother wasn't in the kitchen or living room, and neither Grandma nor her mother played with her. Her mother was usually in the bedroom, and much of the time the door was closed. Sarah sat in front of the TV, watching the stack of videos her mother brought with them.

Sarah, who had always been a very playful and agreeable child, started changing. She alternated between being whiny and clinging, to being uncooperative and having tantrums. Eileen was exhausted by the physical care of her mother, the emotional strain of watching her slowly deteriorate from her debilitating heart disease, and with Sarah's whining and tantrums. At her wit's end with Sarah, she gave me a call.

Basically, the general rule is to discuss with the child what he or she wants. Choice is of primary importance. Not all children want to be present at a death in the home. Not all children want to attend the wake or funeral. They do, however, usually want to be included in the decision. Help your child with choices by making sure that the choices she makes are based on correct information. Sometimes a child won't want to participate, believing it will be frightening. Open discussion about death and funerals often helps alleviate these fears, and your child may change her mind. It will seem less scary if she knows what to expect. If your child still doesn't want to be present for certain events, support this. No one choice is right for everybody.

In the case of Eileen and Sarah, I talked with Eileen about how she was managing all she had on her plate. She was well aware that Sarah was getting much less attention than she was used to, but she thought that there was no other alternative. From her perspective, she was trying to keep things as normal as possible for Sarah.

Eileen and I reviewed possible alternatives to the ways in which Sarah was included. Except for the times spent on personal hygiene, Eileen started keeping the bedroom door open, and she encouraged Sarah to come into the room. Initially, Sarah seemed frightened and refused. It occurred to Eileen to explain the oxygen machine next to the bed and the tubing that ran to her mother's nose. Sarah relaxed some, and at least would stand in the doorway.

Next, Eileen set up a small table with coloring books and crayons in her mother's bedroom and pointed them out to Sarah. Eventually, Sarah chose to join them in the bedroom. As she got more comfortable with the new arrangement, Sarah returned to being her formerly chatty self. Since her mother now slept a lot, Eileen worried that the chatter would be disturbing to her, but the opposite was the case.

When a parent, grandparent, sibling, or other person important to a child is dying, there are usually many ways for the child to participate. For children, like adults, one of the most difficult feelings is that of helplessness. It will help children feel less helpless if they can do something. For young children, this may mean actions as simple as bringing a card, flower, or glass of water to the bedside.

As Eileen watched her mother's pleasure in seeing Sarah nearby as she drifted in and out of sleep, she realized that she couldn't have been more wrong about Sarah disturbing her mother. Sarah had been the light in her mother's life over the past few years, and nothing could give her more joy in her final days than her little granddaughter's presence. Sarah spent much of her time coloring pictures for her grandmother, arranging her favorite stuffed animals around the pillow to "make Nana feel better," and "helping" her mother. They also brought her doll and doll's crib from next door. While Eileen tended her mother, Sarah took care of her sick doll.

The older children are, the more options there are for them to help out or be present. Encourage children to participate in ways that are age-appropriate, and help them take an active role in the end of the life of the person they love. Older children may want to help with some of the physical care their loved one needs. They may want to do things like read to an ill parent, or just sit quietly at the bedside. Include them as much as they want to be included. In this way, you help them learn ways of dealing with many different feelings, including helplessness. And you give them the opportunity to say goodbye in their own way. The key is to give them control of what they can control.

Although I've been discussing the importance of children's involvement, make sure that: the child who does not want any involvement is not responding to fear based on misconceptions, and that older children or adolescents who are electing to have extensive involvement are doing so because it is helpful to them, not because they feel they must. Unless there is absolutely no other option, don't put adolescents in positions of major caretaking responsibility. An adult should take primary responsibility for physical care. However, if your adolescent daughter or son expresses a desire to help in the physical care, support this. They are letting their needs be known.

When children are actively doing something to aid in the

care of the dying person, it can help them manage many of the horrible feelings of helplessness that are stirred up when death is near. Also, participating in hands-on care, helping a loved one get more comfortable, whether by putting on a fresh pillowcase, or lotioning or powdering a back, can contribute to feelings of closeness and caring. Giving care is a way of showing love, and children and adolescents of all ages need the chance to express their feelings in ways of their choosing, before the opportunity is gone.

Helping Children with Choices Surrounding a Death

No one likes bad news. But since we all get bad news at some point, most of us, given the choice, would prefer to have time to adjust to adversity, rather than be shocked by it. There is rarely a good reason to shelter children from bad news. When, for the purpose of putting off the pain of loss in their lives, you shelter children from news about the seriousness of an illness, you rob them of the opportunity to adjust to devastating news, prepare themselves to cope, or share what they would like with the person they love before that person dies.

When death is likely outcome in the course of an illness, children need to be told. When the diagnosis is first made, everyone is frequently invested in the treatment or cure, and, probably, this hope is what you share with the children. But when a prognosis worsens, you need to let them know this, too. You can share whatever is true, even if you're hoping against hope. "Dad's cancer is getting worse, and is spreading. The doctor says there aren't any other medicines that will help much. But we're praying for a miracle and haven't given up hope." Again, don't try to convince them of something you don't believe, thinking this approach is gentler for them. As long as you are honest about what you believe and feel, you will be able to join together in whatever stage the illness is in.

Don't be surprised if your children have a very different reaction than you do. Families are complex, and commonly, each person in a family sees things differently, and will react in keeping with their own age, developmental level, and personality style. The important thing is to try to negotiate the differences so that there is room for each person's way of perceiving and coping with what is happening.

When death does come, listen to your child. What is she letting you know she needs? Help her figure out ways she can be a part of all that is going on. If the death has taken place at home, invite her to view the body, and to say goodbye to the body of the person she loves. It can be very helpful for a child to see that a dead body looks very peaceful. If she protests, don't push it. You may want to ask her if she would like you to tell her what you saw or experienced.

Depending on the age of the child, she may want to help in funeral planning—choosing music, a reading, making or selecting articles to be placed in the casket. Remember, however, that young children haven't mastered the concept of permanence, no matter how well you've explained it. Do not, under any circumstance, allow a young child to place a beloved object in the casket to be buried, such as a favorite blanket or favorite stuffed animal. While this is a loving gesture and may feel good at the time, she will want, and expect, it back later. Of course, this will be impossible. Instead, ask her to think of something that she won't want back later, such as a picture she's drawn, a photograph, or a poem she's written, to place in the casket.

When you take a young child to a viewing, arrange for her to go at a time other than during the public calling hours if at all possible. This way you will be able to give her your full attention, and answer her questions. Be prepared for questions like "How come Grandpa has his glasses on? I thought dead people can't see." If she is going to attend the regular calling hours, assign a friend, or someone your child knows but who is not closely involved, to attend to her. Children can't tolerate intense emotional experiences for long periods, and after being there for a while, she will need to leave and, perhaps, play, or run around to let off steam. If you have an adult assigned to care for her, the two of them can leave together when your child expresses her desire to go.

Older children and adolescents may choose to attend the public calling hours. They too should be encouraged to take breaks as they need—to go outside with friends who come by, or periodically join younger children at play. They also might want to participate in the funeral service by doing a reading, saying something about the person who died, or in some other way. Allow them to choose what kind of participation is right for them, and then support them in their choice.

SEVEN

Lessons from the Dying

Twenty years from now you will be more disappointed by the things
you didn't do than by the ones you did. So throw off the bowlines,
sail away from the safe harbor. Catch the trade winds in
your sails. Explore. Dream.
—MARK TWAIN

Anyone who works in any capacity with the dying knows the familiar response when you tell people what you do for a living. "How can you do that? It must be so depressing!" For each of us, the answer is always the same. "No, it's far from it." There are many, many *very* sad times as people face death—their own and the deaths of the people they love. But it is also a time when what really matters in life comes to the fore.

People who are sick and dying take stock of who they are, and what their life means to them. And as they do, they share themselves in intimate and meaningful ways. As a result, what I primarily experience (and I know this is true for so many others who work with the dying) is gratitude, not depression. Gratitude that people allow me, often a relative stranger, to share in this extremely important time of their lives. Gratitude that I am allowed to witness the power and the strength of the human spirit as people struggle with, and make meaning of, their losses and their lives. And gratitude that I am often reminded of the fragility and value of life.

Over and over again, I see that adversity often pushes us to open up emotionally, share more deeply with those we love, and talk about much that usually goes unsaid. An impending death is often the catalyst for this type of growth—providing all involved with the experience of increased honesty, closeness, and richness in the relationship.

You don't need to wait until the moment when death is staring you in the face to push yourself in this way. Take advantage of the experiences of others, those who are facing their deaths, and incorporate the lessons they have to teach you into your life now. Life is short, unpredictable, and precious. Use the time you have now. If you *wait* to say and do what you want, or don't even take the time to pay attention to what it is you truly do want, you may lose the opportunity altogether.

Control Is an Illusion

Despite our efforts to convince ourselves otherwise, we are not very powerful creatures. In our Western-European culture, we forever strive for control. But the sense of control we manage to get is based more on illusion than reality. About the only control we *really* have is control over our own volitional acts—what we say and what we do. Beyond that, we make our best effort to influence our environments and situations, but mostly, these things are not under our control. When you think about it, this idea is both scary, and at the same time, quite freeing.

Acknowledging a lack of control can help you put your energies elsewhere, rather than struggling to control things you can't.

One of the major problems that comes with struggling to maintain a sense of control is that you tend to get separated from the experience of the moment. You get focused more on the future, and how you might achieve certain outcomes. Setting goals for the future, and working toward them, is of course very constructive and leads to all sorts of accomplishments. But if you let them become your sole orientation, you are likely to pay the high price of losing your focus on the present. You risk not seeing what is in front of you, connecting with those around you, or expressing yourself in ways you want to.

Know What Is Important to You

What most of us need in life is to feel like we are heard or understood. I am always struck by how important it is for people to tell their story—this is one of the main things that people do when they have the opportunity at the end of their life. But, because of our discomfort with death and our need to control and "fix" things that seem wrong or out of control, we can, as listeners, inadvertently obstruct someone's opportunity to tell their story when they need to.

I suppose people who are dying talk to me simply because I will listen, without doing much more than trying to understand their feelings. Rarely do I have answers or words of wisdom to offer, beyond some general information *if* it is asked for—information about common reactions, or different ways in which others handle certain difficulties. But it is just as rare for "answers" to be what is truly being asked for.

What I do have to offer is my firm belief that somehow, through all kinds of experience, people find their way, make some kind of meaning of their losses, adversity, and their lives. It is never a matter of "getting over losses," or even "getting over pain," but, rather, finding ways to integrate the pain as our creativity, our passions, and our losses make us who we are.

Finally, as I listen to the stories of people's lives and imminent deaths, I remember that I too will die. The awareness of this fact helps keep life in perspective for me. It's easy to get caught up in all kinds of worries and plans on a day-to-day basis. As we do, many of these things start seeming *very* important, and our investment in them can take on a life of its own. Tasks we want to accomplish, objects we want to acquire, or petty misunderstandings or arguments can all loom very large.

When I am reminded that my time, and the time of the people I care about, is limited, I stop and ask myself about these things that carry so much weight: "How much does this really matter?" Sometimes I realize that, for whatever reason, it *does* matter to me, and I know I need to focus my energy there. Other times I realize that it doesn't, and I can let it go.

The Value of Humor

Over the years, I have noticed that people who are dying, and those who care for them, often use humor to deal with their situation. There are probably several reasons for this. Humor can help us distance from feelings that are emotionally very intense. How many times have you been part of a very serious and uncomfortable discussion, when suddenly someone cracks a joke, and the entire tenor of the conversation, not to mention mood of the group, changes for the better? Or do you know someone who can only crack jokes, and never have a serious conversation?

BONNIE

I first met Bonnie twenty years ago when I was working as a visiting nurse. She was forty-six and had a degenerative illness; she had lost all of the voluntary function in her lower body and much of it in her upper body. If finger food was placed in front of her, she could eat independently, but getting the food from the plate to her mouth was a daunting task, and as much landed on the bed as got into her mouth. Due to muscle weakness and control problems, Bonnie's speech was difficult to understand. She spent much of every day in a specially designed reclining chair. Because she was a large woman, she needed to be moved from the bed to the chair with the help of a hydraulic lift.

One day, when Bonnie's usual care assistant was out, I went to her residence to get her set for the day. I had known Bonnie for a little over a year and was familiar with her care requirements, but was not often the one carrying them out. After bathing and dressing her, I got the slings for the lift positioned under her, hoisted her into the air, and started wheeling her across the room to her chair. We had been talking and joking some, and as we crossed the room, she started to laugh, which, as it always did, caused muscle spasms. Her body arched. I had positioned the seat sling of the lift too high up under her thighs, so in her arched position, the sling functioned as a slide. Slowly, she started to slip from the lift. I knew I wouldn't get her to the chair before she fell completely, so I did the only other thing I could think of—I helped her to the floor, trying to break her fall.

Unfortunately, I ended up going down with her. In fact, I was pinned underneath her. She was too heavy for me to lift in the best of circumstances, and from underneath her, as we lay on the floor with her sprawled on her back over me, muscles spasming, both of us laughing—which worsened the spasms, I couldn't budge her.

The more impossible the predicament seemed, the harder we laughed. The situation was completely absurd and out of control. (I hadn't been taught the management of this type of problem in nursing school.) It took fifteen or twenty minutes for both of us to stop laughing long enough for her body to relax some, and for me to work my way out from under her.

Humor can make situations that seem frightening or overwhelming feel more manageable or less threatening. Look how often black humor is used in films and theater around issues of death. Sometimes we laugh because it seems like the best choice; we either let ourselves feel the helplessness, threat, or devastation of a situation over which we have no control and no way to protect ourselves, or we laugh.

We laugh at many situations that make us feel uncomfortable. Many of us laugh when we're anxious, nervous, or surprised. Who hasn't had the experience of laughing at a time that seemed inappropriate, either because of the discomfort you felt, or because what you just saw or heard, when removed from its solemn context, was funny? Most slapstick humor involves someone getting hit with something, falling, being startled, embarrassed, humiliated, or being in some way the subject of an unpleasant experience.

I think the humor we see around death encompasses all of these reasons and more. The physical decline associated with dying is often quite undignified. We lose control over of all sorts of bodily functions. And since we are so attached to being in control, we then respond with humiliation and shame. It seems as though we are failing at one of the most basic tasks in life—control over our own body.

Sometimes, though, we have a different response to losing control. These are the times when we are with people we love and trust, and we take a very different view of the embarrassing or humiliating moments—when we step back, and *laugh* at our inability to maintain control. We laugh at the outrageousness of it all. When we can laugh together, it gives us a new way of sharing.

It's so important to share laughter, especially at difficult times, when we need our connections the most. When we laugh, we tend to be very much in the present. We are free to focus on the experience of the moment. We tend to connect with those around us who are also caught up in the moment. Think about how important our social connections are at times that are truly meaningful. It's no wonder that sharing laughter provides us all with such a vital aspect of experience, especially when we are coping with difficult situations.

The situation with Bonnie and myself on the floor could have been a very embarrassing one. No adult wants to be on the floor, pinning their nurse down, completely unable to control their body. Imagine yourself in Bonnie's position. Had she focused on her inability to maintain any kind of control, she probably would have felt a great deal of shame. Instead, it was a time we laughed together. It ended up being an incident that we looked back on often, and made reference to, always with more laughter, for the remaining year of her life. I know she felt closer to me after that, and was able to talk about some of the losses she was struggling with, as her life became ever more limited, and her death nearer.

I also felt closer to her, and always looked forward to seeing her (whereas before this incident, since her care requirements were time-consuming and physically demanding, I had often dreaded the days when I had to fit her into my schedule). I know there were many times when I was caring for Bonnie that she was emotionally down or less than cooperative, but I don't remember any of them very clearly. The time that we laughed together, when my mistake and her physical debilitation landed us both in a bind, however, I will never forget. Still, twenty years later, I remember that time clearly, and think of her warmly.

HELEN

When I was working as a nurse, late one evening shift, Helen, who was eighty-five and in the hospital following a stroke, rang for me. She needed help using the bedpan. I was working with another patient, and Helen, getting no response, and not wanting to soil the bed, decided to take matters into her own hands. With her good hand, she got the bedpan off the side table and attempted to get it underneath her. She was unable to fully lift her hips off the bed, however, so she could only get the pan partially under her. She then tried to scoot herself farther onto the bedpan. Unfortunately, the bedpan moved with her, leaving it still under the back of her thighs. She tried again. The result was the same. Determined to manage, she kept trying to heave her semiparalyzed body onto the pan. With each effort she scooted farther down the bed, and finally, went right off the edge, bedpan and all. Since this was in the days of metal bedpans, she hit the floor with a racket, which got my attention.

The sight of this elderly woman lying on the floor, hospital gown twisted, bedpan at her side, alarmed me, to say the least. Helen appeared to be crying uncontrollably. But it soon became evident that Helen was laughing so hard that her already impaired speech was completely unintelligible, and tears were flowing down her cheeks. Miraculously, she was not hurt.

Helen could have easily responded to her situation with humiliation. Here she was, a usually dignified woman, sprawled across the floor, unable to manage even this simple task. Instead, she was able to picture herself and the absurdity of her situation. She and I, as well as each of her family members she told the story to, were able to join together and laugh on each of her tellings. Being able to laugh with her about her loss of control also helped others join with Helen around this aspect of her experience, rather than pulling away due to discomfort.

As with most aspects of life, if it's important when it comes to death, it is important in life in general. If you can laugh around situations involving sickness, disability, and death, you can laugh at just about anything. With the exception of situations involving abuse or violence, most things have their funny side. Allow yourself to stay entirely in the moment and appreciate this funny side. In this way, you can come together with others in a very basic way; one that is uniquely human.

How Should We Spend Our Time?

Frequently, awareness of our limited time propels us into taking stock of our life choices, and our relationships. When the length of life remaining is clearly limited, the idea of quality takes on new meaning. Oftentimes, the perceived risks in life shift from revolving around what *is* said and done to what *has not* been said or done, for there may be no tomorrow to accomplish what is not done today.

By necessity, prioritizing choices becomes much clearer. For many people, the bottom line is that their relationships play a primary role in giving their life meaning. Often, however, attention to these relationships has taken a backseat to the demands of daily living, or to societal conventions. As people facing death examine their choices, they often realize they *haven't* made the people or things that are the most important to them their top priorities, when it comes to allocating their time or energy. They then shift gears and make different choices.

It is quite common for people near death to describe the final stretch of their lifetime as some of the most meaningful time they have had. It is equally as common for those close to the dying person to describe the time living with the dying person as the best time in their relationship as well. Oftentimes, the only regret expressed is the wish that they had said and done earlier what they said and did at the end. And again, it is so important for us all to remember that we can make choices to maximize the quality of our time, and our relationships, *before* we're facing death in our own lives. Ask yourself the following questions:

- What is important to me, or what gives my life meaning?
- Are the things I value the most the same things that get most of my attention?
- What do I want for my relationships?
- Overall, am I achieving what I wish to?

If you identify areas of dissatisfaction in answering these questions, then ask yourself, "What in my life needs to be different?" Do you recognize any patterns in your life that you don't want to continue repeating? The patterns in our lives seem like they occur due to circumstances out of our control. This may or may not be the case. When it comes to the quality of our relationships, recurring patterns or themes tend to have their roots, at least in part, in the choices we make. We either are choosing the same type of person with whom we interact in problematic ways, or we inadvertently or unconsciously push for the same type of communication or interaction. If we're not satisfied with our results, we have to examine our methods.

Taking Action

If you want your life to be different in ways, you have to figure out how to go about things differently, that is, *if something really matters, give it your attention now.* As we work toward our hopes and goals for the future, we often inadvertently sacrifice our quality of life in the present—more than we intend to. It's important to stop and examine these choices. If you sacrifice, if you work hard, if you give up a lot now and your choices don't get you where you thought you were going, or with whom you thought you were going, will the sacrifices be worth it? Are the steps along the way enough? If not, what— that is in your power to do—would make the present satisfactory in its own right? Would some modified version of your current approach to your life, and relationships, address your needs more completely? It may be time to take some risks.

Our emotional reactions and our behavior patterns are very complex. Sometimes the changes we need to make may seem obvious, but we seem unable to make them. Or the patterns may seem obvious, but there do not seem to be any viable options for change. Still other times, the patterns seem impossible to discern. For any of these situations, it would probably be helpful to work with a professional therapist to examine your motivation, choices, and solutions. We are creatures of habit, and old habits are difficult to break. So don't hesitate to get the help you need for self-examination. You can begin by asking yourself:

- What do I want the people I love to know—both about me and about my feelings toward them?
- Have I expressed these thoughts recently?
- If I were given the information that I had only a few months to live, what would I do differently?
- Are there ways, either minor or major, that I would want to alter my choices or interactions?
- What changes would I make if I were dying? Can I make these changes now?
- What is keeping me from taking these actions?
- What kinds of support do I need to do to accomplish these changes?

Remember that death is not the enemy. It is one of the defining parameters of life. Our fears are the enemy, the cause of our tendency to hold ourselves back, and limit our growth and potential. It is usually our fears that keep us from expressing ourselves fully to those whom we love.

When we talk clearly with those we love about who we are, who they are, and what gives our lives meaning, even if the topics in and of themselves are hard or painful in any way, the overall experience is usually not one of sadness. It is more often that of joy, since in those times we come together closely and experience the greatest gift there is—that of sharing ourselves. We don't need to wait until we are staring death in the face to learn these lessons. We can learn from others and make the most of what we have today. Then, ideally, each of us on our deathbeds will be able to look back and say, "I did my best and made the most of what I had."

Resources

There are many excellent resources available today on all aspects of death and grief. Sometimes it can be difficult to know where to begin. The following list offers a starting point. Many of the resources listed have additional suggestions.

Books

CARE OF THE DYING

Dying Well: The Prospect for Growth at the End of Life. Ira Byock: Riverhead Books, 1997.
> This book, filled with stories by dying patients, offers a hopeful view of dying. The stories illustrate how people experience emotional and spiritual growth during their final phase of life.

Final Gifts: Understanding the Awareness, Special Needs, and Communications of the Dying. Maggie Callahan and Patricia Kelly: Avon, 1997.
> Two hospice nurses describe, through case studies, the experiences of the dying and the meaningful interactions that occur at the end of life.

The Good Death: The New American Search to Reshape the End of Life. Marilyn Webb: Bantam, 1997.
> This book is a journalist's well-researched effort to describe dying in the United States. She uses individual's stories to examine current

law, policy, and common medical practice, and she offers recommendations for ensuring a "good death."

Handbook for Mortals: Guidance for People Facing Serious Illness. Joanne Lynn and Joan Harrold: Oxford University Press, 1999.

Handbook for Mortals is a practical, comprehensive and easy-to-read guide to end-of-life care. It includes suggestions on how to manage physical symptoms of illness, and describes emotional and spiritual issues commonly experienced by the dying.

Share the Care: How to Organize a Group to Care for Someone Who Is Seriously Ill. Cappy Capossela, Sheila Warnock, Sukie Miller: Fireside, 1995.

A guide to organizing and setting up the necessary supports for managing the care of someone who is dying, *Share the Care* addresses the practical details of life, and the emotional demands of serious illness.

Tuesdays with Morrie. Mitch Albom: Doubleday, 1997.

The author, a former journalism student of Morrie, describes the life lessons he learned from Morrie Schwartz as they met weekly while Morrie died from ALS.

Be Prepared: The Complete Financial, Legal, and Practical Guide for Living with a Life-Challenging Condition. David S. Landay: St. Martin's, 1998.

This comprehensive guide, written by an attorney, offers a guide to the practical concerns created by life-threatening illness.

SUPPORTING CHILDREN

How Do We Tell the Children? A Step-by-Step Guide for Helping Children Two to Teen Cope When Someone Dies. Dan Schaefer and Christine Lyons: Newmarket Press, 1993.

This book has excellent information about what children at each stage of development are likely to think and feel about the death of someone close to them.

The Grieving Child: A Parent's Guide. Helen Fitzgerald: Simon & Schuster, 1992.

The Grieving Child offers guidance in such areas as visiting the seriously ill or dying, especially difficult situations, including suicide and murder, attending a funeral, and the role religion can play.

Part of Me Died Too. Virginia Fry: Dutton Children's Books, 1995.

The author, a bereavement counselor, encourages young people to use their creative talents to ease their emotional turmoil: Each of the eleven real-life stories she includes is followed by a selection of reasonable self-help activities—make a trouble doll, stitch a memory quilt, and so forth. The narratives, from young people ranging in age from toddler to teen, encompass a wide variety of situations.

BOOKS FOR CHILDREN

Annie and the Old One. Miska Miles: Little, Brown, 1971. (School age)

When Annie's Navajo grandmother says that when Annie's mother's rug is completely woven, the grandmother will die, Annie tries to hold back time by unweaving the rug in secret.

How It Feels When a Parent Dies. Jill Krementz: Alfred A. Knopf, 1981. (Later school age through adolescence)

Eight children from age seven to seventeen speak openly of their experiences and feelings. As they speak, we see them in photos with their surviving parent and with other family members, in the midst of their everyday lives.

Lifetimes: The Beautiful Way to Explain Death to Children. Bryan Mellonie and Robert Ingpen: Bantam, 1987. (Preschool and early school age)

A pet . . . a friend . . . or a relative dies, and it must be explained to a child. This sensitive book is a useful tool in explaining to children that death is a part of life and that, eventually, all living things reach the end of their own special lifetimes.

Nana Upstairs & Nana Downstairs. Tomie De Paola: G. P. Putnam, 1973. (Preschool and early school age)

Tommy is four years old, and he loves visiting the home of his grandmother, Nana Downstairs, and his great-grandmother, Nana

Upstairs. But one day Tommy's mother tells him Nana Upstairs won't be there anymore, and Tommy must struggle with saying goodbye to someone he loves.

Sadako and the Thousand Paper Cranes. Eleanor Coerr: G. P. Putnam, 1977. (School age)

Based on a true story, a young girl faces the battle of her life when she is told that she has the "atom bomb disease," leukemia, thus she turns to her native beliefs by making a thousand paper cranes so that the gods will grant her one wish to be well again.

The Saddest Time. Norma Simon: Albert Whitman & Co., 1986. (Late pre-school through mid school age)

The Saddest Time explains death as the inevitable end of life and provides three situations in which children experience powerful emotions when someone close has died.

There's a Rainbow Behind Every Dark Cloud. Gerald Jampolsky: Celestial Arts, 1978. (Late school age and adolescence)

Eleven children share their experiences with terminal illness, especially the ways they helped each other cope with the prospect of their own death.

Waterbugs and Dragonflies. Doris Stickney: Pilgrim Press, 1985 (Preschool and up)

Waterbugs and Dragonflies is a graceful fable written by Doris Stickney, who sought a meaningful way to explain to neighborhood children the death of a five-year-old friend. The small book is beautifully illustrated by artist Gloria Ortiz Hernandez.

When Dinosaurs Die: A Guide to Understanding Death. Laurie Krasny Brown: Little, Brown, 1996. (Preschool and early school age)

This reassuring children's guide to understanding death continues the series that includes *Dinosaur's Divorce* and comfortingly addresses common fears and questions while offering sympathetic suggestions for ways to remember a loved one.

Web Sites

Aging With Dignity
>   This site gives directions for purchasing "Five Wishes," an easy-to-use document to help you put in writing your wishes should you become too seriously ill to be able to speak for yourself.
>   *www.agingwithdignity.org*

Americans for Better Care of the Dying
>   This nonprofit organization is dedicated to social, professional, and policy reform to improve care for people with serious illness and their families.
>   *www.abcd-caring.org/*

carethere.com
>   Carethere offers information about advance care planning, family caregivers concerns.
>   *carethere.com*

Growth House: Guide to Death, Dying, Grief, Bereavement, and End of Life Resources
>   This site is an award-winning gateway to resources for life-threatening illness and end-of-life issues.
>   *www.growthhouse.org/*

Last Acts
>   Last Acts is a call-to-action campaign, funded by the Robert Wood Johnson Foundation, dedicated to improving end-of-life care through the sharing information and ideas by professional caregivers, educators, and consumers.
>   *www.lastacts.org/*

On Our Own Terms—Moyers on Dying
>   Here you will find articles on end-of-life issues, a guide to financial planning at the end of life, audio and video clips dealing with end-of-life care, and a state-by-state description of end-of-life related activities
>
>   *www.pbs.org/wnet/onourownterms*

Partnership for Caring
>   This organization offers resources including living wills and medical powers of attorney. (800) 989–9455
>
>   *www.partnershipforcaring.org/*

Organizations

Alzheimer's Association
>   919 North Michigan Ave., Suite 1000
>   Chicago, IL 60611-1676
>   (800) 272-3900
>   *http://www.alz.org*
>
>   The Alzheimer's Association is a national organization that provides information, referral, education and support to people with Alzheimer's disease and their families.

American Heart Association
>   National Center
>   7272 Greenville Avenue
>   Dallas, TX 75231-4596
>   (800) 242-8721
>   *http://www.amhrt.org*
>
>   The American Heart Association offers information and referral services, education, and written materials.

Cancer Care, Inc.
 1180 Avenue of the Americas, 2nd floor
 New York, NY 10036
 (800) 813-4673
 http://www.cancercareinc.org
 Cancer Care, Inc., is a national organization that provides information, counseling, and support to people living with cancer.

Hospice Foundation of America
 2001 S St., NW, Suite 300
 Washington, DC 20009
 (202) 638-5419
 http://www.hospicefoundation.org/
 The Hospice Foundation of America offers resources, education opportunities, general hospice information, and a guide to local hospices.

National Association of People with AIDS
 1413 K St., NW
 Washington, DC 20005-3442
 (202) 898-0414
 http://www.napwa.org
 The National Association of People with AIDS provides information and referral for people with AIDS and their caregivers.

National Institute on Aging
 Information
 P.O. Box 8507
 Gaithersburg, MD 20898-8057
 (800) 222-2225
 This institute provides information and referral services, education, and written materials on aging.

About the Author

A licensed psychologist and registered nurse specializing in death and bereavement, CAROL WOGRIN is the Executive Director of the National Center for Death Education and Director of the Bereavement Studies Program at Mount Ida College. She was recently appointed the Director of the Massachusetts Compassionate Care Coalition, a grassroots organization dedicated to improving end-of-life care. Also in private practice and a frequent public speaker, she lives in Newton, Massachusetts.